The Ride of Our Lives

The Ride of Our Lives

LESSONS ON LIFE, LEADERSHIP, AND LOVE

John Gronski

XULON PRESS

Xulon Press
2301 Lucien Way #415
Maitland, FL 32751
407.339.4217
www.xulonpress.com

Unless otherwise indicated, Scripture quotations taken from the New King James Version (NKJV). Copyright © 1982 by Thomas Nelson, Inc. Used by permission. All rights reserved.

Printed in the United States of America.

ISBN-13: 978-1-6305-0530-1

In memory of
Paul X. Gronski, Sr.
And
Joseph "Jerry" Gronski

ACKNOWLEDGMENTS

I WISH TO THANK THOSE WHO ASSISTED ME WITH THIS BOOK.

To my wife, Berti, whose enthusiasm keeps me going. She is my best friend. To my son Timothy and his wife, Alysa, who one evening while we were sitting around a fire pit, motivated me to tell the story of a remarkable adventure that had happened over thirty-five years ago. To my son Stephen, whose grit and hardiness inspire me. My wife, Berti, and my sons, Stephen and Timothy, have enriched my life and I am thankful.

To Chase Spears, an enthusiastic young man who encouraged me to write this book and graciously assisted with editing. I am grateful to Michael Long for getting me started writing this book and pointing me in the right direction. To my longtime friend Rich Scaricaciottoli, who assisted formatting the pictures that appear in this book and assisting with the design of the front and back covers. To Paul Bracey, a good friend and a renowned outdoor photographer, who was kind enough to review my manuscript. Paul also wrote the *Foreword* to this book. To my Penn State professor John J. Sosik, Ph.D., who provided helpful comments on my manuscript.

To my nephew Anthony and his wife, Melany, who provided valuable feedback.

To my brothers and sisters, especially Ruthie and Ann, who helped raise me. My brothers and sisters have made my life more special. To my Aunt Eve and Uncle Mike, who loved me like a son. To my father, who gave me his love and taught me by his example. To my mother who held me in her arms.

Table of Contents

FOREWORD

FIRST, IT SEEMS APPROPRIATE TO THANK TIMOTHY, THE author's youngest son, for finally talking his father into telling the story in *The Ride of Our Lives*. As with many adventures of this sort, it makes a great story.

Stephen's orange trailer that he rode in as a baby was a fixture in the bike shop at Paul Gronski Enterprises, and while many were aware of what John, Berti, and Stephen had done, the details were always sparse. Here, the gaps of information about this great adventure are filled in, infused with positive energy, a Gronski trademark. Readers who know the author, especially anyone who has tried to keep him in sight while riding mountain bikes, will especially enjoy the self-deprecating analysis of the author's athleticism or his occasional "command decision" about where to camp or take in a spectacular vista. Many of the on-the-fly decisions were influenced by personal encounters along the way. All carry a story, and it's telling.

There are so many aspects to an adventure like this that make it worth telling, from the sheer scale of the undertaking to the astounding variety of landscapes one has to traverse to accomplish the goal, the characters encountered and the strength of character gained, as well as the effort expended. It takes special people, and there are many of them in this story. Top sergeant Tapp, the grand-motherly types out of central casting, the newsmen who knew a good personal interest story when they saw one, the campers and other cross-country cyclists with whom they shared campfire stories for a night or two, and kind and generous strangers, like the Killians, who opened their hearts and homes to these weary travelers with a small child (Christian comparisons invited) all add to this incredible story.

One can easily imagine that Berti had no idea what she was getting into when she met John, but she too is an athlete, and this book is also a testimony to her strength, faith, trust, and resilience. She and John made this journey together with grace, humor, and a desire to share an amazing family adventure that some parents only dream about.

This story might stimulate your interest to take on a challenge or embark on an adventure you never thought possible. Your journey, like the author's, may open doors to meet people and develop great friendships, or it may be a great way to connect with your soulmate and create everlasting memories for you and your children.

This story will renew your faith in humanity. Its underlying message is largely the result of the author's outlook and attitude. Everyone he met touched him and left a mark. If we want to regain our connection with nature and our fellow man, we could begin by having a little faith in our dreams and feel truly blessed by the wonderful people we meet along the way. A little faith can go a long way.

Thank you, John and Berti, for your sense of adventure and for sharing the story of this amazing journey.

—Paul Bracey

Chapter One

The Family That Cycles Together Stays Together

Stephen was always the center of attention. In 1983, if any records were kept, my 15-month-old son, Stephen, had to be the most photographed baby in the United States. Stephen, my wife Berti, and I cycled across the United States on a circuitous route that winded over mountains, across rivers, and through snow, rain, and scorching heat for over 4,000 miles. During our cycling adventure, we came across fellow bikers who were in awe of Stephen. They knew how rigorous spending months on a bicycle and living out of small packs could be. The snow, sun, wind, and rain would take its toll on everyone. People were amazed by how well Stephen was holding up. He was the poster boy for resiliency. I became sick at least three times in the three months we spent on the road. Stephen never got sick, except for the time Berti and I fed him sour milk.

It was 1983. No ubiquitous mobile phones or other devices. No Internet, which meant no email, Mr. Google, or social media sites. The closest thing to connectivity during our cross-country bicycle trip was a public payphone that we would come across now and then in a small town on a dusty back road.

Thousands of cyclists rode their bikes across the United States in 1983. Thousands of cyclists still take off on similar cycling adventures. However, by cycling across America with our 15-month-old son, my wife and I became an anomaly, even to fellow two-wheeled adventurers. Cycling with our baby boy made the trip extra special. When I say special, that, of course, means it also came with special challenges as well as special rewards. Before our trip got underway, during the trip, and after the trip, even now more than 35 years later, people can't believe that Berti and I would make such a trip with a baby. When I mention I bicycled across the USA with my wife, I sometimes am hesitant to include the part about our baby joining us, lest the people I am talking to immediately classify me as insane.

We were not crazy parents. Cycling across the USA was a dream of mine. My wife was very supportive of my dream, and we saw no need to give up on that dream because we were young parents. Berti and I thought of our son as an asset rather than a liability or interference. Our love for Stephen was deep. Berti and I enjoyed the outdoors, and as parents, we decided to include Stephen in all our outdoor activities. That included hiking and cross-country skiing. Sometimes Stephen had to pay for our zeal, such as the time I flipped him headfirst into the snow as I tumbled while cross-country skiing with him on my back. I think Stephen adapted well, and the three of us enjoyed participating in these activities as a family, regardless of the bumps and bruises.

Now, if you ask if our bicycle trip was physically harder because we had our young son with us, the answer is yes. The average weight a cross-country bicycle traveler carries in his or her panniers is about 35 pounds. (Panniers are packs slung across the rear and/or front racks of a bicycle, used to carry gear.) The bicycle usually weighs about another 25 pounds or so. My bike and panniers weighed about 60 pounds. But with Stephen involved, things were a little different. The bicycle trailer Stephen rode in weighed 25 pounds when it was empty. Stephen weighed 28 pounds. Other essentials for sustaining Stephen, such as toys, baby bottles, and disposable diapers, added significant weight to my load. Now, I am willing to bet most people have never had reason to weigh a box of disposable diapers. I certainly had no reason to weigh them until I embarked on our bike trip. By the way, a box of 48 disposable diapers weighs eight pounds. You never know, it might come up as a *Jeopardy* question. So, the extra weight I had to pull made the trip more physically demanding. But as far as Berti was concerned, the hefty load slowed me down so she could comfortably ride alongside me.

Although we loved our son, there were emotional and mental challenges that came along with traveling over 4,000 miles, day after day, for three months, with a baby boy. While Berti and I pedaled our bicycles for over eight hours a day, Stephen was secure in his trailer. We stopped for a few minutes about every two hours, so Stephen could stretch his little legs while we stretched our rear ends. As we pedaled, Stephen relaxed in his trailer, eating, sleeping, and drinking. At the end of the day, Stephen was ready to go. Therefore, we did not always get a chance to relax when we wanted or needed it.

Being a parent is a very special thing. In my weaker moments, I sometimes thought it would be much easier if we did not include our children in our lives. We would have more time to play our favorite sport, pursue our favorite hobby, or spend more time at work. We could spend money on more self-indulgent things rather than on shoes, pediatricians, braces, clothing, and education for our kids. We might even end up with fewer gray hairs, or perhaps more hair since we would not have the safety and well-being of our children on our minds. Emotional challenges do not diminish, even as the baby boy grows to be a man. Our trip through life might be easier, but certainly not as special, just as with our bicycle trip. Stephen certainly made our bicycle trip extra special.

I probably would not have written this book if it were not for my young son joining us on our cycling trip. He is the differentiator to this story, as he made a difference in our adventure. The journey would have been easier without Stephen, but not as memorable. Although it is easy to claim that Stephen made the trip more challenging, one could argue that he was the reason our trip was made more comfortable from time to time. I remember cycling through southern Colorado one very hot 104-degree day. The sun scorched our bodies and we were parched. It was near day's end when we came upon the edge of a small town after biking for hours without the sign of even a small shack. To our delight, we spotted an ice cream stand. We happily stepped up to the window to order. As we propped ourselves up against the side of the building, enjoying our ice cream and squeezing into the shade cast by the small structure, a car pulled into the parking lot. A middle-aged woman climbed out of the car and came walking toward the ice cream stand, casting a glare our way—one of those stares that kind of told you she did not much care for hippies or anyone who looked like a hippie, as Berti and I did. Ignoring her angry eyes, I asked her if she knew where a few cross-country cyclists could camp for the night. She wasn't too helpful until her gaze caught Stephen sitting in the back of his bike trailer, playing with his toes and throwing a smile her way. Her attitude changed dramatically. She invited us to spend the night at her home, just two miles down the road, complete with a home-cooked meal, air conditioning, and a welcomed shower.

As you bike across the United States, you become aware of a grapevine that develops out there on the road among the subculture of cross-country cyclists. Because of the weight I was hauling, we never moved very fast, except for going down steep hills, and even then, I moderated our descents to keep things safer for Stephen. We were passed frequently by fellow cross-country cyclists, but they would chat a bit once they noticed Stephen riding in his trailer. Due to these encounters, word spread about the odd couple bicycling across the United States with their baby. Many times, we bicycled into towns and campgrounds where our reputation had preceded us. Our baby boy was becoming a myth and a legend.

Stephen rode in his trailer for over 4,000 miles across the United States. He began the trip as a 15-month-old and finished as a much older and wiser young man of 18 months. At the journey's end, he had spent 20 percent of his life on a bicycle trip. Stephen sat in his big orange-colored Blue Sky bicycle trailer, facing backward. As

I cycled with that big orange trailer behind me, my focus was on the road ahead, while Stephen's attention was fixed on where we had been. Berti and I would joke about the psychological effect this could have on Stephen, but no side effects ever developed. Fortunately, he never acquired the habit of walking backward.

One day we were having lunch outside of a small grocery store when an older lady with a warm smile, who looked like a grandmother central casting would have sent to a movie studio, came up to us and started to chat. She asked all the same questions we had become accustomed to hearing after spending a couple of months on the road: "Where are you coming from? Where are you going? How many flat tires have you had?" Of course, she made the standard comment of, "Your baby boy is so cute." After about 15 minutes, we said our good-byes as she walked to her car and headed out of the parking lot. We mounted our bikes and headed east, and about 10 minutes down the road, we heard somebody yelling to us from their front yard. It was that same lady. She came running toward us and thrust a handful of disposable diapers into the arms of my wife. She wanted to give us a little something for our trip.

We experienced similar acts of kindness as we crossed the United States. We began to realize that our baby boy helped people to open their arms, their hearts, and their homes to us. It illustrated to me how much more special life is when a child is included. However, along with these heartwarming moments, there were also many struggles along the way. I learned there is no reward without risk, and there is no success without struggle and the resolve to conquer adversity. We had no quit in us. Something kept us going. I think what it came down to is that Berti and I believed in each other and our son, and that is what sustained us. We fed off one another. Iron sharpens iron.

Stephen, Berti, and I shared many adventures along the way on what would become the ride of our lives. Through the course of this once-in-a-lifetime journey, we shared every emotion imaginable, including joy, anger, excitement, and fear. This journey transformed us as we learned many lessons about life, leadership, and love.

Chapter Two

A Sense of Adventure

Even before agreeing to ride a bicycle across the United States with me and our young son, Berti had proven she had a sense of adventure. It was in her blood.

During the American occupation of Austria after World War II, Berti's Aunt Maria met an American GI who was there on occupation duty. He was a young American soldier by the name of Lucky Yates. Maria married Lucky, and they traveled the world together during his career in the Army. Lucky's last duty station was Fort Benning, Georgia. It was there in the military town of Columbus that Lucky retired from the Army and opened an auto repair shop. After all, he had been a mechanic in the Army and learned to fix everything from jeeps to tanks. Lucky and Maria settled down in Columbus, where they built a business and raised a family.

Berti grew up on a farm in Austria, near the town of Schaerding. She attended school in a one-room schoolhouse and spent her free time milking cows and plowing fields. Berti was a teenager when she visited the United States for the first time, staying with her Aunt Maria in Columbus. Berti was captivated by the United States. America offered something she hungered for. The opportunities were unlimited in the vast nation. Berti realized you could fit over 50 countries the size of Austria inside the continental United States.

Berti eventually went to nursing school in Austria and then worked in Schaerding as a registered nurse. However, something about the United States drew her back again. Berti left her home in Austria on April 1, 1980, bound for America. She took up residence with her Aunt Maria and landed a nursing job at Saint Joseph's Hospital in Columbus, Georgia.

I was raised in Moosic, Pennsylvania, a town of about 5,000 people, in the northeastern part of the state. Austria was 3,000 miles away and nowhere on my radar. My grandparents on my mother's side were Irish, and on my father's side, they were Polish. My father was a World War II veteran. After the war, he began to repair cars and opened a garage. I grew up changing tires and driving a tow truck. Like Berti, I learned how to get my hands dirty at a young age. Like Berti, I also had a sense of adventure. I knew there was a big country waiting outside of my hometown and I wanted to explore it. I joined the Reserve Officer Training Corps (ROTC) program at the University of Scranton and commissioned into the Army as a second lieutenant upon graduation. My first assignment in the Army took me to Fort Benning, Georgia.

Fate had brought Berti and me to Columbus, Georgia. Berti's cousin and best friend, Belinda, did the rest. Belinda introduced us in May 1980, and I knew I had found someone special. We fell in love. Berti likes to say she was a sucker for a man in uniform. We were married on a warm and sunny September day in Columbus in 1980. For my part, marrying Berti was the best decision I ever made. Berti really had to have a sense of adventure to marry me. It was not long before the Army moved this newlywed couple to Fort Lewis, Washington, where we would eventually begin the ride of our lives from.

In 1983, when Berti and I began our cross-country adventure, we had been married for less than three years and we were still trying to figure each other out. During our 4,000-mile cross-country bicycle trip, we had some serious quality time to learn more about each other.

Chapter Three

Sounds Like a Plan

At the humble kitchen table, plans are hatched, and important life decisions made. Homes are mortgaged, insurance policies purchased, and weddings planned there. The kitchen table is remarkable.

In the winter of 1982-83, it was at our kitchen table where two important decisions were made. The first decision was to leave Tacoma, Washington, in the great Northwest and relocate to my hometown of Moosic, Pennsylvania. The second decision was a bit more adventurous. We decided to make the trip by bicycle. The trip would be self-supported, meaning that we would carry our belongings on our bicycles in packs known as panniers. We would keep these belongings sparse to save weight. Only one spoon each, no forks, a small pot to cook in, and only one bowl—the pot would serve as the other bowl. I drilled holes into the handles of our toothbrushes; ounces mattered. We would carry our home with us a—two-person backpacking tent and two sleeping bags that could zip together. Our most precious cargo would be our baby, who at the time of our decision was only about nine months old. There was nothing we could do about controlling the weight of this growing boy. We would adjust elsewhere.

Making this kind of trip across the United States had been my dream. I shared my hope of cycling across the country with Berti, even before we were married. Berti saw the romanticism in embarking on such an adventure as much as I did. As a newlywed couple, we would discuss our dream of trekking across the United States on bicycles. Then, one variable in our life changed, and he weighed 10 pounds, six ounces. Stephen was born early on a Thursday morning in March 1982 at Madigan Army Medical Center at Fort Lewis, Washington. The emotional high I felt when first seeing my son Stephen was incredible. It was by far the best day of my life up to that point.

After serving at Fort Lewis for about two years, I left active duty in the Army in the fall of 1982. We stayed in Tacoma, Washington, where I worked as an alcoholism counselor, and Berti worked as a nurse. We enjoyed living in the northwest, but we decided to move to Moosic for a variety of reasons. First, my dad was getting older and I wanted to spend time with him. I also wanted to raise my family near my brothers, sisters, and friends back in Pennsylvania. With the decision to move made, we engaged in a more serious discussion about making our trip east by bicycle.

We were in our 20's and healthy. Berti and I loved the outdoors. Conveniently, we were already on the west coast of the United States. The conditions were set for us. All we had to do was mount bicycles and pedal east. Berti likes to tell me that the reason she agreed to this adventure was that she did not know any better. I think Berti agreed to the trip because we had mutual trust. She trusted that I would protect Stephen and her, and I trusted her opinion. Yes, we had a baby boy, but since we did many other outdoor activities together as a family, we did not see this as an issue. However, we knew there were serious preparations to make to execute this ambitious undertaking.

By early1983, we had made up our minds to cycle across the United States. We were all in. We biked and ran and prepared ourselves physically as we had time. Time was a precious commodity. We both had jobs that did not pay high salaries, so we worked double shifts whenever we could to build up cash. We also had to synchronize our work schedules around Stephen. We chose not to pay for childcare. I usually worked at night and Berti usually worked days, so one of us was always home with our growing baby boy. All this work and baby care cut into our physical fitness regimen. We realized that we would have to start our trip with low-mileage days, building up for longer days and mountainous terrain along the way.

I took on a second job in the winter of 1982–83 which also consumed much of my time. I was hired as a park aide at Mount Rainer National Park. Mount Rainer was a winter wonderland, and I worked in a region of the park known as Paradise. The winter of 1982-83 had record snowfalls, and there was easily over 24 feet of snow on the ground. Berti and Stephen would explore the park while I worked alongside the park rangers. The hearty environment toughened the three of us up, and the anticipation of our upcoming trek was heightened as we listened to park rangers swap stories of their past adventures. The park aide job was fun, and the pay was not bad. According to the government employee pay scale, I was a GS-1 and was paid $4.17 per hour before taxes. I was the lowest rated employee on the government pay scale, but I figured I had to start somewhere. A nice perk was that lodging in the park cabins was available for park aides for $2 per night.

We made a list of equipment needed for the trip and established a budget for procuring the gear. Even though Berti and I were experienced outdoor enthusiasts, there was plenty we had to purchase. We were not blind to the belief that we needed to purchase top-quality equipment for a trip of this sort. Top-quality equals higher prices. We were willing to sacrifice savings to buy the kind of equipment we knew we could count on. One of the criteria in selecting gear was low weight. Unlike purchasing meat at a butcher shop, when it comes to cycling gear, the less weight, the higher the cost.

Our list was extensive and included patch kits, bicycle mirrors, emergency blankets, anatomical seats, padded cycling shorts, jerseys, panniers, new wheels, triple chain-ring cranksets, air pumps, and lightweight tools. The list seemed endless, and the budget kept growing. We also had to purchase a bicycle trailer for Stephen, and we spent additional money on customized improvements to Stephen's trailer.

As soon as Stephen's bicycle trailer was delivered by UPS, I wasted no time in assembling it, hitching it to my bicycle, and testing it. We developed an order of march where I would cycle in the lead, and Berti would bring up the rear. With Stephen sitting in the trailer looking behind, Berti could maintain eye contact and talk to him. What we did not anticipate was Stephen throwing his toys out the back of the trailer. Stephen got a kick out of watching Berti stop her bicycle, pick up the ejected toy, and then race to catch up. It led to our first customization of the bicycle trailer. We went to a tent repair shop, and we had a screen fabricated for the back of the trailer. This screen kept the toys inside with Stephen, where they belonged, and took a lot of stress off Berti.

On one of our test rides, we cycled down a hill into a high school parking lot. I avoided a speed bump with my bicycle, but because Stephen's trailer was slightly wider than my bike, the left wheel of the bicycle trailer caught the speed bump, causing the trailer to tip over. I applied the brakes quickly, and the trailer skidded along the pavement with Stephen inside, secured to his seat with a single seat belt across his waist. Berti jumped off her bike and ran to Stephen's rescue. He was a bit shaken up but had no bumps or scratches. This incident led to our second customization of Stephen's bicycle trailer. We headed back to the tent repair shop and had a four-point shoulder harness added to his seat. This ensured Stephen would stay secured in his trailer if a similar mishap were to occur.

Another high-cost item was a series of maps I purchased from Bikecentenial, an organization founded in the 1970s prior to the American Bicentennial of 1976. The purpose of the organization was to promote cycling. The organization established a bicycle route across the United States known as the TransAmerica Bicycle Trail and published detailed maps of the route. Thousands of cyclists negotiated the route between Astoria, Oregon, and Yorktown, Virginia in 1976.

The TransAmerica Bicycle Trail is not really a trail at all. It is a recommended route for cyclists traversing the United States. The route meanders primarily through the rural countryside where automobiles, trucks, and cyclists all share the road. As a 20-year-old, stories of those who had made this cross-country bike trip and the people they encountered along the way inspired me to cycle across the United States. Bikecentennial published maps of the entire route. We did not plan on following the exact route but intended to ride across portions of it. The cost of the maps totaled $69.03 plus $2.88 shipping. Because the Internet did not exist, I placed my order the old-fashioned way—I mailed in the order form along with a check.

Berti and I decided to bike with a purpose, raising money for the Scranton Boys Club. The Scranton Boys Club held a special place in my heart. I grew up just outside of the city of Scranton, Pennsylvania. I played basketball with a group of friends every winter at the Scranton Boys Club from my freshman through my senior year of high school. I was a poor basketball player, possessing very little athleticism, but I loved playing at the Boys Club with my friends. I had grown up in a mostly white community. Playing at the Boys Club opened the door to friendships with a more diverse group of people. This was a formative step in my youth that began to open my eyes to the world beyond my neighborhood.

A man named Jerry refereed our games. I think Jerry felt sorry for me because of my inability to score points. One evening, during my third basketball season, I fouled an opponent by hacking him on the wrist as he went up for a shot. Jerry stopped the game and awarded me with the "Hatchet Man Award." The actual award was a red wooden hatchet, made in the Boys Club woodshop. The inscription explained that I was awarded the hatchet in honor of my 1,000th career personal foul. We named our team the James Gang, after a high school friend named Ruthie James, who attended most of our games. We jokingly referred to Ruthie as the owner of our team. My time at the Boys Club was a highlight of my teenage years, and I felt an obligation to give something back to the Boys Club.

WARM AM radio was the most popular radio station in northeastern Pennsylvania while I was growing up, with tens of thousands of listeners and well-known personalities spinning vinyl all day. A few months before Berti and I began our bicycle trip, the radio station caught wind of our proposed journey and contacted me. They asked me to call into the station every few weeks for live interviews over the course of the journey. I thought this was a cool idea and readily agreed. Little did I know that Berti, Stephen, and I would become regional celebrities. Years after the trip, people still stopped us to ask if we were the ones who had cycled across the country as a family.

One of the final acts of trip preparation was to sell both of our vehicles. I drove a small 1980 Datsun pickup truck. It was the first new vehicle I had owned, and I loved that truck. Berti, Stephen, and I enjoyed many overnight camping trips with that 4x4 pickup. I ended up selling it for $6,900. My wife drove a white Chevy Vega. That car brought in $250. A coworker at the detox unit where I had previously worked drove the Vega away with a promise to mail a check to my address in Pennsylvania. I am still waiting for the check. That $250 would add up to an incredible amount now if I figured in interest.

On May 27, 1983, three days before Berti and I started to pedal toward Pennsylvania, I sat in our apartment in Tacoma, laid bare of furnishings. Movers came and made short work of packing our furniture and placing it onto a Mayflower moving van. Our furniture would arrive in Pennsylvania months before we would. I performed final mechanical adjustments on our bicycles. I worked on the bikes all through the night and never slept, probably more due to nerves than workload. As I pulled that all-nighter, adjusting brakes and gears on our bicycles, Berti worked her final graveyard shift. The evening before, 10 of her fellow nurses treated her to a going away party at a fancy Mexican restaurant. Berti would soon burn through those calories as we embarked on our human-powered journey.

Jerry Heller from WARM radio contacted me for our first interview on May 27. He got right down to business and asked me, "Why are you doing this?" I did not have a good answer because frankly I really did not know. I told him this had been on my mind for a long time. It was a personal dream. I decided to stop dreaming and start doing. That was the best answer I could come up with. He also asked what my greatest concerns were. I told him there were two: the traffic and the extreme changes in the weather we expected to encounter.

Berti and I prepared as much as we could for our epic adventure, even as we worked and cared for Stephen. There was only one more thing to do, and that was to start pedaling. That is what we did on the morning of May 30, 1983. We did not stop until we reached my hometown of Moosic, Pennsylvania, three months later, on Berti's birthday, August 27th.

Chapter Four

THE FIRST DAY

YELM—A LITTLE FARM TOWN IN WASHINGTON STATE.
It was complete with a general store, a junkyard for farm tractors, cows as far as the eyes could see, and best of all, a gentleman farmer and his wife who happened to be our very good friends. This was where the first day of our trip across our vast nation brought us— Alvin Tapp's farm.

Alvin was a retired United States Army first sergeant. First sergeants in the United States Army are respected by enlisted soldiers and officers alike. They usually answer to the name "Top." This is a term of endearment for the highest-ranking noncommissioned officer in a company-sized unit, which can range between 120 to 350 soldiers. Alvin was not only a first sergeant, but he had been my first sergeant, and he had certainly earned my respect.

Alvin was about five feet, eight inches tall and probably weighed about 145 pounds. He was small in stature but had an enormous heart. Alvin had been retired for less than a year. After transitioning out of the Army, he immediately bought a farm in a rural area south of Tacoma, Washington. He wanted to live a simple life. Alvin loved his wife, Linda Joy, who was about 20 years younger. Linda Joy was a petite young lady, but she had a heart as large as Alvin's. She wanted to raise sheep and knit wool sweaters. This was what caused "Top" to purchase the farm. In my mind, it was kind of like the vintage television show *Green Acres*, but Alvin and Linda Joy were determined to make farm life work for them. Alvin insisted we spend our first night on the road at his farmhouse. I am glad he did. We spent two nights at his home in Yelm as we struggled to get our lactic acid-laced legs under us.

We arrived in Yelm just past noon. Thirty miles and about three and a half hours earlier, some friends and neighbors had gathered in front of our modest two-bedroom apartment in Tacoma to see us off. Our apartment was bare, but our hearts and heads were full of anticipation. I handed the apartment key to our landlord and received a pat on the back and the obligatory words, "Good luck." Berti, Stephen, and I exchanged hugs, kisses, and handshakes with those who had come to see us off. Stephen received most of the hugs and kisses, and then into the trailer he went. Promises were made to stay in touch. Out of the corner of my eye, I noticed some of our well-wishers shaking their heads, probably doubting our judgment to make this audacious journey. I am sure there were thoughts of other adventures that had gone awry, such as the Donner Party's winter spent in the freezing Sierra Nevada Range and Robert Scott's ill-fated South Pole expedition.

As we headed out, the weather was overcast and cool, but I was thankful we had no rain. It was kind of strange to start pedaling away from the apartment we had called home for the past eight months, knowing that we were now out there on our own, just the three of us. Rather than the thrust of an internal combustion engine, we had to rely on our own legs to power the trip. We did not have a steel frame of an automobile's chassis and body to protect us. We were the ultimate thin-skinned vehicles. Those thoughts passed through my mind as we began our adventure in earnest. There was no turning back. We had burned the ships, just as Cortés had done in 1519.

The first day of our epic bicycle trip was also the first time we rode with our full "combat load." Up until this time, we had not done a trial run with all the gear and supplies loaded onto the bikes. This was discovery learning. Within one block from our apartment, I began to have doubts about whether I had prepared enough. I had to stop and tighten my seat post because it had loosened and begun to wiggle and slowly sink down into the bicycle frame. About 20 feet later, I had to stop again because the heel of my right foot kept hitting my rear pannier. The gears on my bicycle were clattering and not fully engaging. That made matters worse. This was a little embarrassing. I felt sure Berti's confidence in me must be eroding as I worked to overcome these rookie mistakes.

I did not tell Berti at the time, but as we cycled out of Tacoma, I was fighting with my bicycle to keep it going in a straight line, and this struggle continued until we reached Yelm. I was as wobbly as a four-year-old riding for the first time without training wheels. The load felt much heavier than I expected. I found out a few days later that Berti had felt the same way, but she said nothing. We both silently dealt with our self-doubts. We did not talk very much for those first 30 miles.

Our route that first day took us from Tacoma into Lakewood, across Interstate 5, through the McChord Air Force Base housing area, through Tillicum and the Madigan gate into Fort Lewis, then along a rural road through the towns of McKenna and Roy. The traffic was sparse and cooperative. We took this as a good sign. Berti and I noticed many strange looks from people passing us in their cars and from pedestrians along the roadside. That was not a good sign, although we should have expected it. We were a colorful sight with yellow panniers slung from the front and rear of our bicycles and a bright-orange trailer that resembled a Conestoga wagon.

As we pulled into Alvin Tapp's driveway, there was my loyal first sergeant standing out front to greet us. I was happy to see him and just as happy that we could stop at his house for a night or two. After this 30-mile struggle, I knew I had to make some adjustments, so I got right to work.

The first thing I did was offload the panniers from my bicycle, and I detached Stephen's bicycle trailer. I loaded this bike, that had to carry me and my son across the country, into Alvin's well-worn pickup truck, for a trip to Stevenson's bike shop. The mechanic at Stevenson's installed a more compatible and smaller front chainring and adjusted the derailleurs so that the gears shifted smoothly.

I had read a ton of books about long-distance bicycle touring in preparation for our trip. Unfortunately, I did not always heed the advice of what I read. That was about to change after our experience of that first 30-mile leg. Those first 30 miles on the road taught me how important a well-balanced load was. I remembered reading that the panniers on both sides of the bicycle had to be of equal weight. The books recommended that I weigh the panniers on a scale. It had seemed like a great deal of fuss, and I did not have a scale, so I skipped that step. At Alvin's house, I asked to borrow his bathroom scale and was meticulous in ensuring the panniers on both sides of our bikes were of equal weight. This was no time to mess around.

I had foolishly and carelessly thrown cans of soup, fruit, and noodles into our panniers before beginning the excursion from Tacoma. I now jettisoned the canned goods. I left Alvin with enough canned food to get him through the month of June. I figured since we would be cycling on roads, albeit rural roads, we would always be within striking distance of a grocery store or restaurant. We were not hiking in the outback. We did not have to carry a pantry with us, and we wouldn't starve. In my quest to save weight, I made a difficult decision and left my juggling bean bags at Alvin's house too. I would have to find other ways to entertain myself at the end of a long day of cycling.

After repacking, Berti and I did a test ride for a few miles with Stephen in tow. The difference in how our bicycles handled was dramatic. My bike shifted precisely. The load was lighter and properly balanced now. We were rocking and rolling. We regained our confidence. All it took was paying attention to detail. An expedition of this nature had to be executed properly if we were to succeed. Our eyes were opened, and I was thankful we had our friend Alvin's house as a safe harbor to work out some bugs.

Berti and I awoke on the morning of June 2nd full of anticipation. I did a short interview with Jerry Heller at WARM radio. The questions came quickly: "What kind of roads will you be traveling on?" "What do you expect your progress will be?" "How are your wife and the little guy doing?" I don't think my answers were very good, probably because my mind was on our upcoming travels. All I wanted to do was get the trip started again. Then we were off, well-rested and a bit wiser.

Chapter Five

With a Little Help
from Our Friends

THE NICE THING ABOUT PLANNING FOR AND CARRYING
out a trip like ours is that it reminds you that you are not an island.
I believe that in order to carry out anything of real significance, you
cannot go it alone. You need others. You need good teammates and
friends. Over the course of our journey, we leaned on old friends
and found new friends to help us along.

After I transitioned from active duty in the Army in September
1982, I began serving with a US Army Reserve unit in Tacoma,
Washington. As in most military units, it did not take long to make
new friends. Most soldiers are like-minded in terms of shared values.
Even though the United States Army is probably the most diverse
institution in the world, the camaraderie is unlike what you find
anywhere else. The "never leave a fallen comrade" culture is unique.
We will do anything to support our battle buddies because we know
they would do the same for us. Thus, I became fast friends with a
fellow Army reservist, Allan Yamamoto.

Prior to Berti and I embarking on our cross-country bicycle trip,
Allan gave me his address and phone number. He lived in Centralia,
Washington, and his house sat along the route we would travel into

Oregon. Allan said he would like to have Berti, Stephen, and me stay at his home along our way. Along with Alvin and Linda Joy Tapp, Allan and his wife, Sharon, were in a long line of beautiful people who opened their homes to us on our extended journey across the United States.

After leaving the Tapp farm in Yelm, on June 2nd, we headed south on State Road 507. The road had a good shoulder to ride on. That was lucky for us. As we cycled along the road, logging truck after logging truck sped by. Logging truck drivers must get paid by the number of flatbeds they deliver, based on how fast they drive. As these trucks rumbled by, the wind they generated whipped at us and pushed us forward. I could only pray the truckers did not swerve onto the shoulder, or we would have been as flat as the roadkill that littered the highway.

When we were not cowering from the rush of these huge logging trucks, we were outsprinting farm dogs. Plenty of dogs gave chase to us along Route 507. I am a dog lover, but these dogs were hard to fall in love with. They had vicious barks and sharp fang-like teeth, glistening as foam dripped from their mouths. They were more like junkyard dogs than farm dogs. We were getting some serious speed work in. At one point, I took my water bottle and squirted one mongrel right between the eyes as he was about to taste my right calf muscle. I was lucky. My aim was true, and the stream of water in the dog's face was enough to turn back "Mutley."

Other than the nine logging trucks and five dogs we encountered (yes, we kept count), the ride went well. The toughest part of the whole day was the last two and a half miles. We turned off Route 507 onto Zenkler's Road, an unpaved gravel road. Our tires sank into the deep gravel, forcing us to walk our bikes the last mile to Allan and Sharon's house. This road was steep, and I had a hard time pushing the weight of the bike and trailer through the gravel. The toil and sweat of negotiating the steep gravel road turned out to be well worth the trouble.

21

We had a great evening at the Yamamoto homestead. Allan was away on business, but Sharon was a marvelous hostess. The house was spacious and well kept, and the countryside surrounding the home was radiant under the setting sun. Sharon prepared lentil soup, salad, and muffins for dinner. I had not known Sharon's husband for very long. I had been in the reserve unit with Allan for only a little over six months. During that time, I saw Allan only one weekend a month. I had never met Sharon before that afternoon when we wheeled our bicycles up to their front porch. Even so, the Yamamotos opened their doors and hearts to us. Sharon treated Stephen like one of her own children. She treated Berti and me like family. The banter around the dinner table was easy. We laughed quite a bit as we told stories about Stephen's first year on earth. Berti and I recounted precious memories of when Stephen took his first step and the first time he waved good-bye to me as I was about to go to work.

We talked with Sharon about what we thought life after our bicycle adventure would bring us. Berti and I had left behind many employment opportunities in Tacoma. I had been asked by the park rangers at Mount Rainier National Park to join their ranks. I had completed firefighter's testing in Tacoma and was placed on the short-list to become a fireman. I was courted by an insurance company to become a salesman, and by an owner of a resort to become a manager. I even took the postal carrier's test. I wanted to keep all my options open. Berti had a promising career as a registered nurse. Despite these opportunities laid before us, Berti and I decided to move back to my hometown in northeastern Pennsylvania and take on a role in my father's business where I would work alongside my brothers and sisters. As in all family businesses, working alongside my family would be a risk, but it was a risk we were willing to take. Though committed to this seismic life change, Berti and I remained a bit apprehensive about what the future might hold. It felt good to discuss our dreams and concerns with Sharon around the dinner table.

Berti and I appreciated Sharon's hospitality. To demonstrate our thanks, Berti washed the dishes after dinner, and I split wood in the backyard, providing tinder for Allan and Sharon's woodstove. I do not know if Sharon knew, but splitting wood was one of my favorite things to do. I was not helping her as much as she was helping me.

Berti and I were at a crossroads in our lives. It was a crossroads between living in the Northwest or living in the Northeast, a crossroads between living away from family or with family. Life is full of decisions like this. In a microcosm, we made many such decisions over the course of this trip. We had to decide such things as, *should we turn east or turn south? Do we stop now for the evening or bike another 10 miles before making camp for the night?* What I found is that no decision is ever the wrong decision. You should never second-guess yourself. The key is how you approach the decision you make. Once you decide, go all in. Move forward energetically and with great enthusiasm. As the last line of the US Army Ranger creed states, "Readily will I display the intestinal fortitude required to fight on to the Ranger objective."

In just our third day of cycling, we were enjoying our adventure. After spending evenings with the Tapps and then the Yamamotos, Berti and I began realizing that the beauty of this trip would not be in the scenery we passed, but in the people with whom we would engage. It is people, not things, who nurture our souls.

Chapter Six

THE GREAT CASTLE ROCK FIRE

ONE OF THE THEMES IN THE MOVIE *FORREST GUMP* was (I will stay G-rated here) *stuff happens*. We all know stuff happens in our lives that we do not expect. What separates success from failure is how we respond.

I've always prided myself on living a healthy lifestyle. Physical fitness is a very important part of my life. I have worked to stay in top physical condition since my high school years. However, at times I could be clumsy. That might explain the cause of what Berti and I refer to as the "Great Castle Rock Fire."

Berti and I were making good progress cycling our way south toward the Oregon state line. We looked toward Oregon with anticipation. We had visited Oregon before and were impressed with its beautiful rocky coastline, so we had reason to believe the interior of Oregon would be just as scenic. Our bikes took us through Chehalis, Washington, and then we cruised through several smaller towns. We decided to have lunch at a grocery store in Winlock, Washington, that seemed to be right out of the 1960s television series *Petticoat Junction*. The grocery store doubled as the county's post office. We passed on the postage stamps and ordered a lunch consisting of pressed ham and rolls. The sandwiches we made were tasty, and Stephen was a big fan of the fresh bread. As we munched away on our sandwiches, I noticed a sign hanging on the bulletin board proclaiming "Egg Day" was only one week away. This hand-made piece of marketing material promised egg breakfasts, deviled eggs, egg salad, blue ribbons, and prizes. It seemed that Winlock kept its chickens busy.

Our goal for the day was to reach a campground at Castle Rock. Upon arriving in Castle Rock, Berti and I discovered the camp-ground we planned to spend the night at was five miles out of our way, and all uphill. We decided to keep moving toward Oregon. As we both pedaled south of Castle Rock, the sun drifted lower in the western sky. We would have to stop soon and make camp. Our new goal was to find a piece of terrain worthy of spending the night. I noticed a farmer working in a field, and I asked permission to camp on his property. He pointed to a corner of a field he had recently purchased: permission granted. The farmer seemed amused by Stephen, sitting in the back of his trailer and gnawing on his favorite toy.

Once we waded into the field, we observed a few cow pies here and there. Stephen seemed bothered by the dry grass that towered about a foot over his head. Otherwise, it seemed to be good ground, espe-cially considering that the sun continued to sink toward the horizon.

Dinner consisted of lukewarm stew. Our Peak 1 one-burner back-packing stove almost caught fire, forcing me to put the stove out before our dinner was fully heated. We were able to supplement the meager evening meal with leftover ham and rolls from lunch. While Berti and Stephen gobbled down dinner, I managed to pitch the tent in the remaining moments of daylight. The tall grass hid our humble camp from the roadway, which was just the way we liked it. Our stomachs were full enough to allow us to settle into our sleeping bags for a sound sleep.

The morning sun brought the promise of another good day of cycling. The camp stove proved more cooperative for cooking oat-meal and boiling water for hot coffee than it did for preparing dinner the night before. It looked to be the beginning of a great day until I got clumsy. Just as our pot of water reached a boil for our second cup of coffee, my left foot kicked over the camp stove. This sun-drenched carefree morning immediately turned chaotic. White gas began to run out of the toppled stove, the flame from the burner wasting no time setting the dry grass ablaze. The wind howled from the west and fanned the flames, expanding the fire. The flames shot up about eight feet into the air and singed my eyebrows.

Everything seemed to move in slow motion. I had the sense that my life flashed before my eyes. Then we flung into action. Berti righted the stove, and I put my firefighting skills to the test. My only chance was to create a firebreak by stamping down on the tall grass, and that is exactly what I did. It worked. The fire fizzled out after burning only a few square yards of the field. It was a frantic way to begin our morning. There was no fire or smoke damage to our tent, sleeping bags, bicycles, or to Stephen's trailer. Stephen did not recognize the seriousness of the situation. We had a hard time getting him to stop laughing at our antics.

It was a hard lesson to learn, never to light a leaky, white-gas camping stove in the middle of a field of tall, dry grass. I shake my head when I think this was a lesson I had to learn. We checked in with the farmer before continuing our way. I told him about the fire. Since he had just purchased the land and had no crops growing in the field, he had no problem with a few feet of tall grass catching on fire. The farmer was glad I was able to extinguish the fire without sacrificing several acres of his land. I sometimes wonder if he ever let another cyclist camp in his field again.

Chapter Seven

The Sisters

Having lived in the Puget Sound region for about two years, Berti and I always kept an eye east toward Mount Rainier. From October to April, a glimpse of the mountain was rarer than a fresh vegetable in a drought. Then, without warning, the clouds would clear, revealing a magnificent view of Rainier. We welcomed the beauty of the mountains spanning Washington and Oregon, but we were apprehensive about meeting the "Sisters."

Continuing south from Tacoma toward Oregon, one thought pulsed in our minds—the Cascade Mountains. The Cascades would present what Berti and I considered our first test. We had not cycled in the mountains leading up to our adventure and expected difficult climbs. The mountains would test us in stride. If we could not hold up under the strain of pulling baby and all the accouterments through the Cascade Mountains, our epic voyage would end almost as quickly as it began.

We crossed into Oregon on June 4th on a bridge spanning the Columbia River at Longview, Washington. Steel grates on each end of the bridge had spaces the width of our bike tires, creating a nasty obstacle. We did not want to risk getting our tires stuck in the grates, so we walked our bikes over the grates. We realized we would have to remain alert to hazards like this over the course of our journey.

We met many other long-distance cyclists in Oregon and each of them had a story. There was a couple in their 20's, heading for Canada. They were going to meet some friends from New Zealand at the Canadian border and then continue to Banff. Their trip started in San Diego and they had been on the road for seven weeks when we met. They were enamored with Stephen, taking pictures of our star traveler and his bright-orange trailer.

We pushed through Rainier, Oregon, and met a helpful fireman who recommended that we spend the night at the Big Eddy campground. We took his advice and were glad we did. At our overnight stop, we met Craig, a cyclist bound for Canada. Craig told us he planned to traverse Canada from west to east, ending up in New England. Three years earlier, Craig and some friends cycled from Pittsburgh, Pennsylvania, to Portland, Oregon. Craig told us that in his 1980 cross-country adventure, he had grown to love people because he encountered so many nice and helpful folks on his journey. He arrived in Portland with three dollars in his pocket and no place to stay. Craig took the first job he found, which was as a busboy at Rosie's Restaurant. He soon rose to the rank of a waiter. After three years of waiting on people at Rosie's, his love of humanity became tarnished. Now Craig was back on a cross-country cycling adventure, hoping to rekindle his love for mankind.

We continued our journey east and the next town we came to was Pittsburgh, Oregon. Pittsburgh consisted of one café and one traffic light. There were no intersections, but there was that one light. Next, we entered Verona, a small logging town. We stopped at a grocery store and replenished our supply of disposable diapers, purchasing a box of 12 for $2.49. While in the store, I noticed there was a five-cent deposit on aluminum cans. Oregon was an environmentally conscious state, and the five-cent deposit on aluminum cans was Oregon's way to incentivize recycling and help reduce litter. In my capitalistic mind, I thought this program could partially fund our bicycle excursion. I put together a great plan, or at least I thought so. I asked Berti to get off her bike to retrieve every can I spotted along the roadside. Berti agreed grudgingly, but the execution of my grand scheme was short-lived. After I insisted that Berti stop her bike in the middle of a climb up a 15 percent grade, she revolted. That ended my idea to fund our trip, and I never suggested a plan like that again.

As we cycled east from Verona the terrain changed from timber-based to agrarian, and we spun through some very pretty countryside. Besides the scenery, another benefit was the disappearance of those large, speeding logging trucks. These mammoth trucks were replaced with something much more appealing—strawberry stands. It seemed like there were strawberry stands everywhere now. For lunch, we had a pint of ice cream topped with fresh strawberries. Later in the day, we treated ourselves to cottage cheese mixed with strawberries. We were in strawberry heaven. Stephen was in his element. He munched on strawberries while Berti and I chugged along through the beautiful rolling hill country.

We made our way into the town of Yamhill, Oregon. Main Street was decorated with quaint stores and shops. Victorian homes sporting well-manicured lawns lined intersecting side streets. Several church steeples added to the ambiance. There were no campgrounds in sight as darkness settled upon us. I remembered reading in a book that churches were generally a safe place to camp if all else failed. Berti and I were both Catholics, so when we spotted a Catholic church on the outskirts of Yamhill, we believed our prayers had been answered.

I knocked on the door of the rectory to no avail. I left a note for the priest, and we pitched our tent in what seemed to be a perfect location, between the church and the parish hall. There was a bonus: the restrooms behind the parish hall were unlocked, so we had a place to use toilets and wash up. Yes, our prayers had been answered, or so I thought. About 9:30 p.m., as Berti, Stephen, and I nestled into our tent, there was a strange noise. I crawled out to investigate. A man came around the corner of the church hall and bumped into me. He identified himself as the parish priest. He wore loafers, brown socks pulled up on his calves, Bermuda shorts, and a polo shirt. He tried to control his anger as he stammered, "May I ask what the meaning of this is?" As he spoke, he brandished a flashlight in his right hand and shined it at my face and then toward our tent. I explained that I was cycling across the United States with my wife and 15-month-old son. I described how the sun was setting and that we desperately needed a place to pitch our tent for the evening. I offered the weak defense that I left a note on his front door. The priest was quite irritated and proclaimed that I was "presumptuous." However, he was lenient in that he said we could spend the night since we already had our tent pitched and the baby was sleeping. As a fellow Catholic, I was taken aback by his angry demeanor. The next morning, we broke camp quickly and were on our way again.

We cycled into Dayton next, a slow-moving little town with a park adorned with fresh colorful flowers. As Stephen entertained himself at the playground, Berti and I entertained ourselves by eating sticky buns and drinking orange juice purchased at the village bakery. Following this break, we negotiated scenic roads and traversed a bridge above the Willamette River into Salem. Oregon's capital city, with a population of 90,000 people at the time, was the biggest city we had ridden through thus far. We replenished the calories we had burned by sharing a meal under a shade tree in front of the local humane society building. I managed to cut a cantaloupe in half with my camping knife and Berti and I each filled our halves of the tasty fruit with cherry yogurt. It felt like a feast. It was under the shade tree that we decided to take Route 22 east into the Sisters Mountains rather than cycling south into Eugene. Other cyclists we spoke to promised beautiful scenery along that route. We looked forward to the beauty of the mountains, but we also steeled ourselves for some demanding climbs.

The next few days brought challenges along with the gorgeous countryside. We ran into a great deal of truck traffic along Route 20. There was a wide shoulder to ride on. However, wind blast from passing semi-trucks hit us hard as they roared by. The reward for enduring Route 20 was a stay at an Oregon state park overlooking Detroit Lake, a forest-ringed canyon lake in the Cascade Mountains. The park offered a great view of Mount Jefferson, which was shrouded in snow and looked like a bride's veil. There we met a wonderful young woman in her 20's, who with her teenage nephew, was cycling from Portland to Philadelphia, Pennsylvania. They knew the rigor of cycling long distances and were amazed at how well Stephen was holding up. We also met Joe Stewart, a jovial fellow in his 60's, retired and now serving as the Detroit Lake State Park host for the month of June. He proved to be an excellent host and invited us to his camper for coffee, a welcome invitation given our current nomadic lifestyle.

Hal and Kim Gypson were our next-door neighbors at the Detroit Lake campground. Both were retired, making the best of their golden years, touring North America in a Volkswagen Vanagon. Nine years later, in October 1992, I received a card in the mail from Hal. He reported that Kim passed away in 1990, but not before they visited most of the United States, Canada, and Mexico. He had many memories, including two pictures he mailed to us along with his notecard. The pictures were of three crazy cross-country cyclists, including a 15-month-old, enjoying themselves at Detroit Lake State Park. Hal's card brought back memories of swimming and playing in Detroit Lake amid the beauty of the Cascades, experiences made richer thanks to our campground neighbors Hal and Kim.

After leaving Detroit Lake State Park on June 8th, we encountered the Three Sisters, closely spaced volcanic peaks in the Cascade Range of central Oregon. The nearest town is Sisters, Oregon, about 10 miles north of the peaks. This first day cycling in the mountains would also be our day to challenge Santiam Pass. Old survey maps showed Native American trails passing through Santiam Pass. In time, these trails became routes for explorers, trappers, and wagon trains. It was cool negotiating terrain covered by our forefathers from the 19th century. The elevation at Detroit Lake was about

1,500 feet. We would reach an elevation of 4,817 feet before this day of cycling concluded. The steep route to the summit was tough, though Berti and I never had doubts about making the climb.

Before reaching the summit, we pulled up to Lost Lake Campground. The campground was closed because it was early in the season and snow still covered the ground. Near the campground entrance, we took the opportunity to rest and eat. We were getting low on water after our climb, and I could not find potable water, even though I hoofed it into the campground and scouted around. I briefly thought about melting snow. After further thought, I decided the situation was not critical enough to spend time melting snow, and I believed we would come across a water source soon. We pressed on.

That was our last rest before pushing on to the summit. At the crest, we found a Presbyterian church camp and youth hostel, so we pulled in to check it out. The living quarters were plain and spartan. A man in his 20's who claimed to be the manager's friend, briefly showed us around. There was not much to see except for piles of snow that still lay on the ground after a long winter. The most valuable thing I found was a water faucet, and I greedily filled our water bottles to the brim. The climb, even in the cool weather, brought Berti and me to the point of dehydration. We refilled Stephen's sipping cup with his favorite drink—cherry Kool-Aid.

After conquering the summit, we started a six-mile descent. It was as frightening as it was exciting. When it was over, our hands and feet were numb from the cold air which felt even brisker because of the wind chill created by our speed as we careened down the mountain. The large piles of snow we had cycled by at the summit decreased in size as we plummeted downward, and then we coasted into the town of Sisters, Oregon. The view of the snowcapped mountains surrounding Sisters was incredible. Our hearts were beating fast from the beauty around us and the adrenaline rush from the descent. We were jubilant. We had managed to climb our first summit and survived the downhill ride. We were now seasoned veterans of the TransAmerica Bicycle Trail.

Chapter Eight

Herman

THE DISTANCE BETWEEN OREGON AND BELGIUM IS approximately 5,000 miles. It was at Sisters State Park in central Oregon that Berti, Stephen, and I met Herman De Lael, a young Belgian, a continent and ocean away from his hometown of Beerse, Belgium.

The Sisters State Park campground had seen some wear. The picnic tables and shelters all needed a coat of paint. After our climb over Santiam Pass, we also showed some signs of wear. However, we were not in need of paint. Rest was what we wanted. Sisters State Park would be our home for the night and would provide the needed place to rest.

As I was setting up camp, the evening of June 8th, I met a tanned cyclist with leathery skin who appeared to be well worn too. It turned out he was 67 years old. This aged wonder had begun his trek in Michigan, and his destination was his daughter's house in Salem, Oregon. He was full of advice. He recommended I ditch the red flag I had hanging on the back of Stephen's trailer because of the wind drag it created. He suggested that if motorists could not see a large orange bicycle trailer, they would never see a small red flag. The logic about the size of the flag versus the size of the trailer was sound, but I felt the argument about the wind drag made no sense. The weight of the trailer, Stephen, disposable diapers, and all the other necessities required when traveling with a baby caused enough drag without worrying about a small flag. I still took his advice and threw the flag into a trash can. I did not like it anyway. I also decided to get rid of our bicycle chain and padlock. We had not used it since we began our trip, and I was happy to get rid of excess weight. I kept the lock, for the time being, hoping to sell or barter it at my first opportunity.

Berti and I met another adventurer at Sisters State Park, but rather than traveling by bike, he chose hiking boots. He was in his 20's and started his backpacking trek in Renton, Washington. He began hiking the Pacific Crest Trail but left the trail because, according to him, it was too difficult to carry enough food to get him through long stretches in the wilderness. He had just spent a couple of days at an artesian spring near Sisters and now was bound for Yuma, Arizona. After hiking for the past two months he already wore out two pairs of hiking boots.

Later that evening, Berti, Stephen, and I crawled into our tent. Berti and I were looking forward to falling into a deep sleep, but Stephen beat us to the punch as he drifted off and breathed restfully. I soon heard a ruckus nearby, and I hurriedly scrambled out of the tent, ready to defend our turf. That is when I met Herman. Herman was a bearded fellow, mid-20's, with long unkempt hair. He was struggling to pitch his tent in the dark, so I lent a hand. We became fast friends. Like everyone else, he had a story to tell, and I was all ears.

Herman had flown from Belgium to New York City about six months earlier. His goal was to cycle the perimeter of the United States. He had cycled south along the east coast from New York to Florida. Once in the Sunshine State, he turned west. When he reached the Southwest, he turned his bicycle toward Oregon. He was now on his way back to New York City by way of Yellowstone and the Great Lakes. Herman thought the United States was amazing. I did too.

When the sun rose the next morning, I all got a better look at Herman, and I saw Herman's bicycle for the first time. His bicycle was a spectacle. It was an old, heavy, three-speed bike. While most long-distance cyclists used a triple chainring and 15 gears to negotiate the varied terrain of North America, Herman was cycling the perimeter of the United States with only three gears. Herman's bicycle sported big balloon tires. Heavy handmade leather bags were fixed to the side of his bicycle with leather straps in order to carry his gear. He also had a handmade large metal switchboard mounted to his handlebars to turn on and off a series of lights he had mounted on his bicycle. I thought Herman had to be a glutton for punishment to travel all those miles on such a contraption. Then I glanced over at the orange trailer attached to my bicycle and realized Herman was not the only one who gorged himself on punishing endeavors.

For the next week, Berti, Stephen, and I cycled the same route as Herman. We would usually break camp at about the same time every day. We would start out at about the same speed. Then we would reach some hills, and Berti and I would begin to outpace Herman. We would see each other at day's end. Herman would usually arrive at our campsite about two hours after we arrived. That is when we would share stories about the day's events. Inevitably, we would also share a few laughs.

There came a point when Berti and I parted ways with Herman, as we chose different routes through Oregon. Herman planned to end his adventure in New York City, where his perimeter tour had begun. We talked about the route he would take as he closed on New York and figured there was a good possibility he would cycle through my hometown of Moosic, Pennsylvania. I jotted down my sister Ruth's name, address, and phone number on a piece of paper and pressed it into Herman's hand. I told him if he made it to Moosic, to look my sister up and she would provide a roof and a meal for the evening.

We were disappointed when Herman biked off in a different direction. He had been a good companion. My Austrian wife was happy to have the company of a fellow European, if only for a short time. I was still amazed about the progress Herman made on that 10-ton three-speed of his. He was not the most efficient cyclist, and it took him longer to log mileage, but somehow, he always managed to reach the same destination as we did at the end of the day.

As Berti and I journeyed across America, we took pictures with an old color-film camera. From time to time, I would stop at a post office and mail the film to my sister Ruth, who would get the pictures developed. One day in early August, Ruth was driving along Route 11 in Moosic, when her nine-year-old son began screaming excitedly, pointing out the car window at a grungy-looking cyclist. He yelled, "Mom, Mom, there is the guy in one of Uncle John's pictures!" Ruth turned the car around and approached the cyclist, who was resting near the side of the road. The unkempt cyclist held out a worn piece of paper. When Ruth saw her name, address, and phone number scribbled on the paper in my handwriting, she knew she was face-to-face with Herman. Once Berti, Stephen, and I arrived in Moosic at the end of August, we were surprised and happy to learn that Herman did indeed spend an evening at my sister's home, complete with a home-cooked meal. That was the magic of the TransAmerica Bicycle Trail.

Chapter Nine

Just Another Bull Story

SOMETIMES A HELPING HAND COMES OUT OF NOWHERE
when you least expect it and it is needed most. We were eye to
eye with the beast, and it was seeing red. The timing couldn't have
been better.

On Thursday, June 9th, we found our way to a private campground
across the road from Ochoco State Park. The camping fee was
only $4 and included hot showers. A bonus was great tasting hot
chocolate topped with whipped cream served at the campground
grille. While sipping our hot chocolate, Berti and I met two cyclists,
Diane and Shawn, who were bound for the east coast. These two
cross-country adventures seemed to be focused on covering ground
as quickly as possible. As I crawled out of our small tent the next
morning, Diane and Shawn had already broken camp and were on
their way.

It was a dreary Friday morning, and a hard, cold rain was falling.
Because of the foul weather, we ate breakfast in the camp restaurant.
I gobbled down biscuits and gravy while Berti and Stephen enjoyed
scrambled eggs and ham. Berti and I washed down our breakfast
with hot coffee. We knew we required solid sustenance for what
looked to be a wet and cold day ahead.

Although it was raining steadily, we wasted no time breaking camp after breakfast. Berti kept Stephen busy, staying out of the rain in the laundromat while I did my best to stow our rain-soaked tent and other gear. I shuttled our stuff to our bikes, which I leaned against a wall under a roof near the restaurant. The last thing we wanted to do was sleep in wet sleeping bags that evening. We had one last cup of hot chocolate in the warm restaurant, and then we snuggled Stephen into his trailer with an extra blanket and a large plastic bag. We donned our red rain jackets and then we were off.

We had no rain booties or toe-clip covers to keep our feet dry and warm. The only things between the cold rain and our bare feet were thin cotton socks and cycling shoes. We cycled in the rain for about an hour, knowing we had another 30 miles to go before we reached Mitchell, Oregon, our destination for the day. We pulled off to the side of the road as the wind whipped around us. Berti checked on Stephen. Thankfully, he remained dry and warm. The smile on his face told us he was not aware of the miserable weather. Berti and I munched on a berry pie and Pop-Tarts between chattering teeth. Before we continued, we stood in the rain, sucked it up, and pulled on wool socks, arm warmers, and wool gloves. Once we put ourselves together, our condition improved and so did our spirits.

We cycled for another hour and felt good. The weather had begun to clear. We started a climb and made it to the summit of Ochoco Divide, an elevation of 4,720 feet. We were rewarded by a seven-mile descent into a valley decorated with green pastures. Near the end of the downward grade, some guy in a pickup truck traveling up the mountain tried to flag me down. Because of the weight behind me, I couldn't stop until I had traveled about another hundred feet where the road leveled out. I waited for Berti to catch up with me. Berti told me she had stopped and talked to the guy in the truck. According to Berti, he said, "Be careful; there is a puddle ahead. Go fast."

The rain had subsided but turned to a thin, foggy mist. Steam was rising from the road. We were stopped along the side of the road, trying to make sense of the message Berti had received. As we pondered the message and chewed on raisins and peanuts, we stared at the road ahead. Then we realized what the pickup-truck driver was trying to convey with his mysterious words. As we peered through the mist, we could make out a large animal rounding a curve in the road. Now we understood the garbled message. The guy had said "bull," not "puddle." "There is a bull ahead."

We stood by our bicycles, chewing on those peanuts, staring at the bull. The bull stared back, and he kept moving toward us. We tried to devise a plan of escape, and we knew we did not have a lot of time. I remembered reading that General Patton said something about an imperfect plan implemented today being better than a perfect plan executed tomorrow. Based on our situation, I couldn't have agreed more. Since we had a hill to our backs and level terrain to our front, I felt the best course of action was to climb back up the hill until we could turn around and use the speed generated by our descent to rush past the bull. Thank God, we did not have to execute that imperfect plan.

Out of nowhere, a large blue Dodge pulled up alongside us. An old man rolled down his window. He was dressed in a flannel shirt and wore a soiled green baseball cap. I assumed he was a local farmer. The first words out of his mouth were, "Looks like you are in a bad situation." We nodded. He had hit the nail on the head. Meanwhile, the bull was getting closer. I really got worried because the bull began pawing its hoof at the road, and it was blowing steam out of its nose. I thought that only happened in cartoons. Berti and I quickly took off our red rain jackets. We did not want to provoke the bull more than it already was. The farmer took charge. He told us he would lead us past the bull, keeping his large blue Dodge between us and the beast. The bull was getting closer and looking meaner by the second, so we had no choice but to stop talking and start acting. The farmer drove at about 10 miles an hour, and Berti and I kept the Dodge between the bull and our precious cargo in my bicycle trailer. Once we passed the bull, we cycled along with the car for about another mile before we all came to a stop. I wanted to hug that farmer, but he never left his car, probably because he did not want to be hugged by some skinny wet guy on a bicycle.

Berti and I put our bright-red raincoats back on once we survived this ordeal and the bull was safely out of sight. We were both shaking, and I am not sure it was entirely from the cold weather. We checked on Stephen, and as usual, he greeted us with a big smile. We thanked the farmer, said our good-byes, and then offered a prayer of thanks to our Creator whom we knew had watched over us. That rural road we were cycling on was desolate. Before the guy in the pickup truck flagged us down, we had not seen another car for about 30 minutes. I do not doubt that divine intervention brought that farmer in the blue Dodge our way at just the right moment. You cannot tell me miracles don't happen.

Chapter Ten

All in a Day's Ride

CHALLENGES AND REWARDS, FIRE AND WATER, HEAT
and cold, good and bad. So goes life and so goes the experiences
one finds on the TransAmerica Bicycle Trail. It is all what you
make of it.

A deer glided through the woods and vaulted a downed tree with
the grace of a ballerina as we entered the town of Mitchell, Oregon,
late in the afternoon on June 10th. We bedded down at a youth
hostel to end a day of cycling that had packed a lifetime of experiences into an eight-hour period. We had climbed mountains,
encountered hair-raising descents, come face-to-face with a bull
that outweighed me tenfold, met a guardian angel dressed as a
farmer, cycled through fossil beds, and breezed past landscapes that
mirrored the Badlands. We had a great day.

In Mitchell, there were signs posted throughout the town warning
visitors not to drink the water. We never found out what the
problem was, but we heeded the advice of those postings. Stephen
drank cow milk here rather than powdered milk, and canned juice
rather than Kool-Aid. Berti and I went the Gatorade route.

The youth hostel in Mitchell featured graffiti, boarded windows,
and broken doors but offered hot showers and a well-equipped

kitchen. For dinner, we popped pot pies into the oven, and I treated myself to two cans of Hamm's beer. Breakfast consisted of Grape-Nuts cereal since we had to use up our fresh milk. We added sweet buns and coffee from a café across the street before mounting our bicycles to start our day.

We cycled out of Mitchell on Saturday morning and were immediately surrounded by red canyons. Reaching the small town of Dayville, we snacked on cottage cheese and apples for lunch. We found a small park for Stephen, and he enjoyed himself playing on the jungle gym in the playground. We continued through Oregon at an ambitious pace.

At that point, we had been on the road for a couple of weeks. Our legs had grown lean and mean, and we continued to meet the nicest and most helpful people. We arrived at Clyde Holiday State Park and were greeted by our cycling friends Diane and Shawn. They waved us over to their campsite and had five juicy cheeseburgers waiting for us. Local folks were having a picnic at the park, and they were happy to share their food with a group of cross-country cyclists. When you bicycle over 60 miles a day for weeks on end, you never turn away a cheeseburger. Lately, I had been eating like a horse. Blueberry pancakes, Yum-Yums, oatmeal, omelets, bacon, cherry pies, stew, ice cream, and fruit all went down easy, and it did not take long to burn those calories.

We cycled through idyllic towns dotting the countryside with names that dripped with the legends of western settlers. We cycled through John Day, Prairie City, and Unity. When we arrived at Unity, I had the strangest feeling that I had ridden into a town out of the pages of a Louis L'Amour paperback novel. Unity was trapped in a time warp. I swore I was back in 1870. Unity was nestled in the mountains, and when I awoke in the morning at our campsite just outside of town, I had to scrape frost from our panniers before I could retrieve the camp stove. The water in our bottles was coated with a thin layer of ice. This was our coldest night on the trail. Some hot water and a couple of cups of coffee and hot chocolate reduced the chill and got us moving.

Before leaving Unity, I found about 20 empty Miller beer cans. With Oregon's bottle bill, these cans were worth five cents apiece. Unfortunately, when I presented the cans to the grocery store in Unity, the manager would not accept them because they did not have the words *Oregon Refund* stamped onto the top of the cans. I placed the cans in Stephen's bicycle trailer, figuring another store along the route might accept them. As we traveled with the cans in the trailer, Stephen had a good time kicking at them. He occasionally would manage to knock a can out of the trailer, forcing Berti to stop and retrieve it. I could hear Berti grumbling every time a can hit the pavement. Finally, in Brogan, Oregon, I found a grocery store willing to pay a bounty on the cans. I cashed the cans in for what I considered to be a big haul—$1.15. I was thrilled, but Berti was even happier since she no longer had to stop and pick up the cans Stephen threw at her. Stephen was the only one who was disappointed since his aluminum "toys" had disappeared.

After several weeks on the road, I noticed we were becoming celebrated among the subculture of our fellow cross-country cyclists. People decide to cycle across the United States for as many reasons as there are types of bicycles. Some are running away, and some are running toward. I think for Berti and me, it was a little of both. Word spread quickly that two parents were cycling from west to east with a baby. Even among a group of unusual people, we were not usual. Not many folks tackled the challenge of cycling across the United States with a baby in tow. Cyclists traveling in the opposite direction from us would flag us down when they spotted our bright-orange bicycle trailer. Cameras would pop out and Stephen would be the center of attention as people snapped his picture. Stephen, at 15 months old, had his own paparazzi. Stephen ate this up and always had a smile for the cameras.

Life is one crossroads after another. So goes a cross-country bicycle tour. On Father's Day, June 12, 1983, Berti and I decided to take a more southern route across the United States. Rather than cycling through the Tetons and Yellowstone, we decided to travel through Idaho, Utah, Wyoming, and then south into Colorado before turning east into Kansas. Berti and I had traveled through the Tetons and Yellowstone a few years before, so we thought we would explore a different route home. Throughout our cross-country bike journey, we were faced with countless decisions about which way to go and which path to take. What I learned was that the path we decided upon was always the right one. It was not so much about which path we chose, but how we chose to negotiate it. It was all about attitude.

Chapter Eleven

The Declo-Longmont Connection

SOME OPPORTUNITIES ARE A LONG SHOT. BUT IF YOU want to stay in the game, sometimes those long shots are worth taking. Sometimes the long shots work out. My dad used to say, "Every dog has its day, even me."

In Adrian, Oregon, we crossed the Snake River into Idaho on June 14th, and we were bolstered by crossing another state line. We bucked a strong headwind all day, and at Keeney Pass, we faced hills that made our quads squeal as they drowned in lactic acid. Our goal was Caldwell, Idaho. We reached Caldwell as the sun was dipping behind the mountains, we recently conquered. We found a place to stay for the night at the Coffee Grounds Campground. Coffee Grounds was a fitting name. It was a rotten little place, privately owned. The price for one night's camping was one of the steepest we paid at $7.75. Our choices were limited, and although we relished the opportunity to shower, it was difficult to stand the stench from the bathhouse as we washed ourselves of the day's grime.

We left at 6 a.m. the next day, anxious to put the campground in our rearview mirror. We passed through the three small towns of Middleton, Star, and Eagle before cycling into Boise. Boise was one of the nicest larger cities we encountered, and we were treated to a complimentary stay at a luxury Holiday Inn. I do not have all the details, but somehow, my brother Robert back in Pennsylvania, worked with Holiday Inn to obtain several complimentary nights of lodging during our trek across the country. We took full advantage of our luxurious accommodations. The hotel boasted swimming pools, hot tubs, saunas, and clean hot showers. We used them all. After being kind to our bodies, we were equally kind to our stomachs and pigged out on fresh sandwiches, nachos, prime rib, and cold beer. Stephen ordered up some chocolate milk. We really splurged.

As we cycled through Idaho, every day brought new adventures. We cycled out of Boise and headed southeast toward the town of Mountain Home paralleling the Oregon Trail. The historic Oregon Trail spanned the distance between Kansas and Oregon and was developed by trappers and fur traders in the first half of the 1800s. Initially, it was only passable by foot or horseback in most parts, and eventually, the trail was traversed by wagon trains. It was very cool to cycle through areas that were once only accessible to pioneers. We cycled on Interstate 84 for about 40 miles. Our legs were moving like pistons in well-oiled machines and we made good time. Our progress was halted momentarily as Berti's rear tire went flat. Like a highly trained Indy 500 pit crew, I had Berti on the go again in under two minutes. From Mountain Home, we traveled on back roads that paralleled Interstate 84 into the small town of Hammett and then took another back road to Three Island Crossing State Park, near Glenn's Ferry. That is where we bedded down for the night. The next morning, we stopped for a welcome cup of coffee in Glenn's Ferry, and a newspaper reporter hunted us down. He interviewed us and took some pictures. Stephen's face was prominently splashed on the front page of the *Glenn's Ferry Pilot*. The young lad was making us famous.

When we left Glenn's Ferry, we rode on Interstate 84 again. It was hard riding as we encountered a strong headwind. We left Interstate 84 at Bliss, Idaho and cycled along U.S. Route 30, a route

46

known as the Thousand Springs Scenic Byway. We wound along the Snake River and encountered some gorgeous scenery, cycling past postcard-worthy waterfalls. The cloud cover disappeared, and a 90-degree sun beat down on us. The sun scorched our bodies as we passed acres of fields with freshly planted crops. As Berti and I gazed at the irrigation sprinklers spraying the fields, we turned our eyes toward each other simultaneously. Our thoughts were in sync. We took the opportunity to cool off under the comfort of a showerhead spraying water into the farmer's field.

We ended our day in the town of Buhl. We received permission from the local police to camp at the town park and baseball field. However, we had to wait until 10:30 at night to pitch our tent because a series of Little League Baseball games were in progress. At least we had some entertainment. The next morning, we cycled toward Burley, Idaho, on a frontage road, that suddenly turned to gravel. We had to bounce over the gravel for about a mile until we were on pavement again. In Burley, we asked the local police for permission to camp in the local park. To our surprise, the police denied the request. We had no choice but to cycle an additional 10 miles to a KOA at Declo, Idaho.

In Declo, before reaching the KOA, we stopped at Judy's Cross-Roads Café. Judy's was an eatery with red-checkered curtains on the window, comfortable tables, and waitresses with quick smiles and playful banter. The chef was a master with his flat-top grill. I enjoyed a tasty veal cutlet, and Berti ordered her favorite meal, liver and onions. Stephen assisted us both in wolfing down the fare. The main courses were topped off with mashed potatoes, gravy, green salad, soup, rolls, coffee, and pudding for dessert. Our bill totaled $8.

It was at the KOA campground in Declo where we met the Ellises, a couple in their 60's who were motorcycling across the United States. The greeted us with huge smiles and asked us to share a meal and drink around their campfire. They told us all about their son, Larry, who lived in Longmont, Colorado. Larry loved to mountain bike and rock climb. Mrs. Ellis insisted on giving me Larry's address and phone number. We expected to cycle through Longmont on our way to Pueblo, Colorado, and we promised we would visit Larry if the opportunity presented itself. I was not sure how likely this would be since Longmont was several weeks and over 600 miles from our current location. I shoved the paper with Larry's phone number into the bottom of my handlebar bag.

The next morning was frustrating as I ran into all kinds of problems changing a tube on Stephen's trailer. I tried to install three different tubes, but they all had holes. I am not sure what caused the problem other than it may have been a defective lot of tubes. Because of the aggravation, we stayed tethered to the campground all day, except for the 25-mile round trip bike ride to the town of Burley I had to make in search of a 24 x 1 3/8 bicycle tube for the trailer. Burley was a small town, and there were no 24-inch tubes to be found. I ended up purchasing a patch kit and repaired the tube rather than replacing it. This was not my preferred course of action, but the repair held up.

We left the Declo KOA about 8 a.m. on June 20th after a healthy breakfast consisting of shredded wheat, strawberries, nectarines, and milk. We enjoyed some good riding. The wind was at our back. The roads were relatively flat, although we did climb over Sweetzer Summit which had an elevation of 5,530 feet.

We crossed the state line into Utah and ended our day at the small town of Snowville. We camped near a baseball field adjacent to a firehouse. We met the first cyclist we had seen in over a week. Mike was cycling from Colorado Springs to Seattle on a Specialized Stumpjumper. He pitched his tent near ours and then joined us for a cup of coffee and relaxed conversation. Visiting with fellow travelers was becoming our favorite way to spend an evening.

As we continued through Utah, we cycled through Bear River, only 20 miles from where the Golden Spike was driven into the rails of the Transcontinental Railroad in 1869. We cycled through Brigham City and felt the Mormon influence around us. We had stopped for strawberries at a roadside stand when a family in a pickup truck pulled up and began to talk to us. They were Jerry and Karen Carr. They had two daughters and four sons, and Karen was pregnant and due in October. They were Mormons. They invited us to stay at their house, and we accepted. Their home was charming. Prior to eating dinner with the Carr family, we had a relaxing swim in their pool. Berti, Stephen, and I slept in a hide-a-bed in their family room. The next morning, Karen prepared breakfast burritos. The only price I had to pay for the food and hospitality was listening to Jerry talk to me about the Mormon religion. A small amount to pay for an enjoyable overnight stay with people who welcomed us into their home and shared what was inside their hearts.

As we cycled toward Ogden, we stopped at a coffee shop for two cups of coffee to go. As we loitered outside the coffee shop, sipping our coffee, the owner came out to chat with us. Before we were on our way, he offered us a free refill on the coffee. He also handed us a bottle of water for our young traveler. We continued to meet bighearted people, and this barista was one of many.

In Ogden, I installed four new tires on our bicycles and a thorn-proof tube on Stephen's trailer. Better to be safe than sorry. We continued toward the Wyoming state line, cycling through Utah's Weber Canyon. Weber was a trapper killed by Native Americans in the 1800s. The canyon we passed through was also traversed by the Donner Party. This was a popular corridor, as Mormons and the Pony Express had also used the route. The area offered a relatively easy pass through the Rockies. The climbing was surprisingly easy, and the snowcapped mountains, fast rivers, and red canyons were easy on the eyes.

We arrived in Echo, Utah, and stopped at a roadside café that was popular with truckers. The owner of the café offered to let us camp behind the establishment free of charge. We gladly accepted the offer. As we left Echo the next morning, a train made its way past us and sounded its whistle as a greeting. We realized why the town was named Echo as the sound of the whistle bounced off the canyon walls around us.

From Echo, Utah we cycled into Evanston, Wyoming. We were happy to cross another state line, but the physical strain of the trip began to take its toll. Berti and I both came down with severe head colds, although Berti held up better than I did. According to Berti, men are big babies when they get sick, and that's probably exactly how I acted. Stephen was also under the weather. He got cranky and vomited twice. I won't go into a lot of detail, but it wasn't pretty. Berti discarded the powdered milk, believing it may have gone bad in the 90-degree heat. Stephen was a hardy guy and bounced back quickly. I was not as tough, and I got weaker by the day. It was my turn to vomit. We checked into the Sunset Campground, and after a hot shower and a day's rest, I recovered. For lack of another good route, we cycled along Interstate 80 in Wyoming. The shoulder of the Interstate was very wide, and we never felt threatened by the traffic. In Oregon, we cycled through the Sisters Mountains and now in Wyoming, we again had to climb over the Three Sisters Mountain Range. These mountains accounted for three long climbs, but after a month on the road, it was nothing we couldn't handle. We were in the heart of the Rocky Mountains. After defeating The Sisters, we cycled into Fort Bridger, named for frontiersman Jim Bridger. The fort was also a Pony Express stop. We spent the evening at the Lyman, Wyoming KOA.

We left Lyman on the morning of June 28th and almost immediately met two other cross-country cyclists. They were Ernie and Tanya, a couple in their mid-30's who became our cycling companions for the next few days. We spent our days cycling together and spent our evenings sharing a meal, sometimes a beer, and all the time we enjoyed some laughs. Stephen also got along well with our new companions. On June 30th our cross-country cycling group spent the evening at the Arlington KOA. The next day we continued to cycle together, reaching Laramie, Wyoming. We enjoyed a hearty meal at a Mexican restaurant together, celebrating our crossing of the Rocky Mountains. After our feast, we bid farewell to Ernie and Tanya. Our new-found friends headed east to Cheyenne. Berti, Stephen, and I were turning south into Colorado. After spending the night at the Laramie KOA, we awoke the next morning and were on the road as the sun rose. We followed U.S. Route 287 South and crossed into Colorado, enjoying the beautiful sight of red canyons to our east and snow-capped mountains to our west. We reached Fort Collins at days end.

The next day a calamity occurred on Shields Road between Fort Collins and Loveland, Colorado. Berti's mind wandered, and she hit the back of Stephen's trailer as we were cycling and tumbled over her bicycle. Berti hit her head hard against the roadway, but her bicycle helmet absorbed the blow. Her elbow was bleeding, but a little first aid saved the day. After assessing the damage to Berti, which ended up being minor, we evaluated the damage to her bicycle. This was also minor. Her front wheel was slightly bent, and I straightened it within a few minutes. Berti's rear pannier was scraped up but still functional. This minor fender bender was a wake-up call, and Berti and I were taught a lesson on the value of wearing a bicycle helmet.

On July 3rd, we approached Longmont, Colorado, riding on Route 287. The road was narrow with very little shoulder. The Independence Day traffic was bumper to bumper. This was not our kind of cycling. Out of desperation, we pulled into a parking lot of a 7-Eleven store to get out of the traffic and take a breather. Cycling in the congestion was very stressful. I then thought back to that friendly motorcycle couple we had met in Idaho over 600 miles ago. I rifled through my handlebar bag and retrieved the address and phone number for Larry Ellis. My hopes were not high as I dialed the payphone. When the voice on the other end of the line identified himself as Larry, I explained who I was. I was greeted with a whoop and a holler. Larry was hoping we would call. His parents had told him all about us. I explained to Larry which intersection we were at, and it turned out we were within three blocks from his home. Larry drove over to the 7-Eleven and escorted us back to his house. He introduced us to his wife, Marge, and his three children, and they graciously invited us to stay with them over the Fourth of July holiday. We were happy to accept the invitation.

We had a wonderful time over the holiday period with Larry, Marge, and their children. Larry loved the outdoors, so he took us to Boulder on July 4th. He was well versed in the trail system there, and we did some hiking. I think Stephen enjoyed the opportunity to break up our cycling trip with a trek through the scenic trails surrounding Boulder. The scenery was spectacular and the conversations we had with Larry and Marge about the lifestyle they chose in Colorado were an inspiration to us. They had fulfilling careers, but they managed to put their children first. They chose to connect their family through the outdoor activities they engaged in. We returned to the Ellis residence as it was getting dark. The timing was perfect, as the local Independence Day fireworks show began. In the Ellises' front yard, we had a perfect view of the light show. The fireworks were some of the best I had seen, and I knew by Stephen's excited screams and laughter that he enjoyed the colorful exhibition.

The stop in Longmont was just what we needed. When Mrs. Ellis handed me Larry's address 600 miles earlier, we never dreamed we would have a wonderful time in Longmont with five wonderful people who seemed more like family than strangers.

Berti Gronski cycling through the Cascades.

John Gronski chugging along with Stephen in tow.

A happy family at Detroit Lake State Park in Oregon.
Photo by Harold Gypson.

Berti finishes securing Stephen in his bicycle trailer before hitting the trail at
Detroit Lake State Park in Oregon. Photo by Harold Gypson.

Berti and John cycling along a rural road as Stephen rides in his trailer.

Stephen sleeps in his trailer as John and Berti take on another hill.

Stephen Gronski, 15 months old, secure in his bicycle trailer.
This photo appeared in the *Wichita Eagle-Beacon* newspaper.

Red rain jackets keep John and Berti somewhat dry on a rainy day.

Berti and Stephen cool off in a stream on a 104-degree day near
Olney Springs in southeast Colorado.

Stephen checks out the campsite in the morning sun.

Lazy Louie cradles Stephen in his arms.

The front side of the Lazy Louie Bicycle Camp postcard.

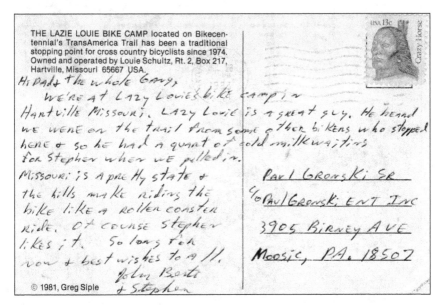

THE LAZIE LOUIE BIKE CAMP located on Bikecentennial's TransAmerica Trail has been a traditional
stopping point for cross country bicyclists since 1974.
Owned and operated by Louie Schultz, Rt. 2, Box 217,
Hartville, Missouri 65667 USA.

Hi Dad + the whole Gang,
    We're at Lazy Louie's bike camp in
Hartville Missouri. Lazy Louie is a great guy. He heard
we went on the trail from some other bikers who stopped
here & so he had a quart of cold milk waiting
for Stephen when we pulled in.
Missouri is a pretty state +
the hills make riding the
bike like a roller coaster
ride. Of course Stephen
likes it.   So long for
now + best wishes to all.
            John Berti
            + Stephen

© 1981, Greg Siple

USA 13c
Crazy Horse

Paul Gronski Sr
% Paul Gronski Ent Inc
3905 Birney Ave
Moosic, PA. 18507

A note John wrote to his family on the backside of a Lazy Louie postcard.

59

This picture appeared in the newspaper at Southern Illinois University.
Photo by David McChesney.

The family enjoys some shade in Kentucky. You can get a glimpse of the
sheepskin bicycle seat cover on John's bicycle.

Berti rides a horse at the horse farm of David and Diane Walsh
in Falmouth, Kentucky.

Stephen gets friendly with a pony at the Walsh horse farm in Kentucky.

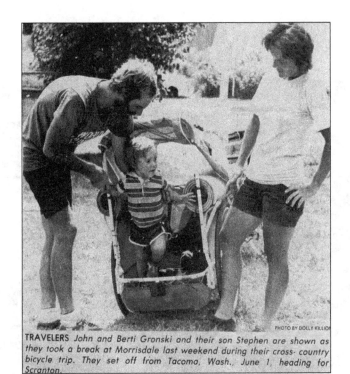

TRAVELERS *John and Berti Gronski and their son Stephen are shown as they took a break at Morrisdale last weekend during their cross-country bicycle trip. They set off from Tacoma, Wash., June 1, heading for Scranton.*

PHOTO BY DOLLY KILLION

This picture appeared in the *Morrisdale Progress* newspaper, Morrisdale, Pennsylvania. Stephen looks ready to explore his surroundings.

John, Berti, and Stephen reach their destination in Moosic, Pennsylvania, after cycling over 4,000 miles.

A crowd of over 1,000 friends, family, and media gather around John, Berti, and Stephen, welcoming home the family of cross-country travelers.

A proud grandpa, Paul X. Gronski Sr., presents grandson Stephen
with his first bicycle.

From left to right: Stephen, Berti, Paul Gronski Sr., and John
share quality time at the welcome home celebration.

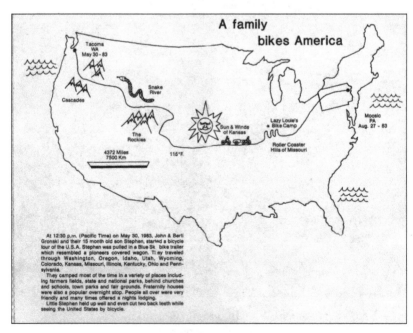

A cartoon sketch of the Gronskis' route across America.

John, Berti, and Stephen, smiling after the trip's successful completion.
The Pittston, Pennsylvania, newspaper, *The Sunday Dispatch*,
ran this picture on the front page.

Chapter Twelve

INVISIBLE HILLS

I HAVE FOUND THAT SOME OF OUR GREATEST CHAL-
lenges are unseen. We must be prepared for anything. It is much
easier when we face these unseen challenges together rather
than alone.

I burned my backside badly. I sat on the sidewalk for a moment
in Pueblo, Colorado, when we stopped for a break, and I paid the
price. That white sidewalk was sizzling in the 104-degree heat. As
we cycled out of Pueblo heading east, the terrain was flat, but the
heat was unrelenting. We stopped in the shade often. Somewhere
between Boone and Olney Springs, Colorado, we sat in a small
stream flowing under a wooden bridge. It is amazing how simple
things like an eight-inch-deep creek can become so precious.

When we arrived at the fringe of Ordway, Colorado, a Dairy
King drew us in. As we licked ice cream cones, Alberta Franzman
approached. She was a lady in her mid-60's, and when she spotted
Stephen in his trailer, her heart melted faster than our ice cream in
the hot sun. She invited us to spend the night with her. She had
a mobile home in her backyard, and she let us have the run of the
place. The shower and the air conditioning were refreshing on a very
hot southern Colorado day. People like Alberta would continually

present themselves to us just when we needed them most. Divine intervention came our way again.

We awoke at 4:45 a.m. on an already hot July 10th morning. We said farewell to Alberta Franzman at 6:15 a.m., attempting to beat the heat and winds, but to no avail. From Ordway, it was the towns of Sugar City, Haswell, and Eads, and then the Kansas state line at Tribune. Between Sugar City and Haswell, there was nothing–no water, no people, no shade, no nothing. We battled heat and wind the entire way. Headwinds and powerful crosswinds harassed us as we penetrated western Kansas. We expected Kansas to be an easy state to cycle across with its terrain as flat as a pool table. We did not expect the powerful winds that amounted to invisible hills. Psychologically, the winds were much tougher to handle than the mountains we had faced. At least we were able to see the mountains. Facing our invisible foe through Kansas was a mind game. Even when we rested, the winds continued to blast at us. To give us a break, I would take my poncho and string it up to act as a windbreak. I was willing to try anything to get some relief from the wind. The wind, pounding our bodies with 20 to 30 mile-an-hour gusts, tired us out even when we were off our bikes and trying to rest.

Then the locusts attacked. It was an assault of biblical proportions. The year 1983 was the year of the seven-year locusts. The swarms of locusts were so thick that they blocked the sun, and we had to place handkerchiefs over our mouths to prevent us from swallowing them as we breathed hard against the unforgiving wind. The locusts were all over us, covering almost every part of our body and our bicycle panniers. We were thankful that Stephen had a screen on the back of his trailer to keep those locusts from attacking him. After the heat, the wind, and the locusts, we wondered out loud if there were still seven more plagues to come our way.

The towns in this part of Kansas seemed to be spread out about every 30 miles. In between towns, there was not a tree in sight. It was not until we came to a town that we were greeted by trees, and we hungered for the shade they provided. I was not a fan of the terrain. I loved mountains and trees, and the Kansas we saw provided no mountains and very few trees. A constant in every town was a grain elevator. As we got within 10 miles of a town, grain elevators would present themselves for the first time, off in the distance. Sometimes those last 10 miles were the longest miles of the day. It was mid-July, and harvest crews were on the roads, moving from farm to farm harvesting wheat. We had to share the road with convoys of combines and other farm equipment.

On one particularly tough day, just west of Hutchinson, Kansas, we were burning in the sun and fighting against the wind, making every pedal stroke an effort. We came upon a Wendy's restaurant, aka Wendy's fast-food hamburger joint, and to us, it looked like an oasis. As we walked into the Wendy's, the air-conditioning soothed our overheated bodies. It was high noon. We decided to order the buffet. It was a healthy choice featuring plenty of fresh fruit and vegetables. After two helpings from the chow line each, plus another child-sized plate for Stephen, we were not about to enter the inferno outside the restaurant door anytime soon. Stephen was more than happy to busy himself with the indoor child-play area.

After about three hours of basking in the air-conditioning, Berti and I filled our plates from the buffet again. For the price of one meal, we had several. The manager and staff did not seem to mind. During a slow period in the early afternoon, the staff became Stephen's playmates. The manager asked us questions about the trip, wondering out loud how we had made it this far, and his eyes twinkled with amazement when we explained how far we had to travel before our adventure was over. Finally, as the sun began to melt into the sky over the Rockies, we made our way out of the restaurant and onto our bikes. The hiatus did our bodies good. The late afternoon became cooler, and even the wind died down. We were heading east again.

We arrived in Hutchinson on July 15th and spent the night at the Zion Lutheran Church house, run by Pastor Bob Woods. At this point, the chamois in our biking shorts had begun to wear thin, and our backsides began to ache. We visited Harley's Bicycle Shop. The shop was phenomenal. It was huge and offered a large selection of bicycles and everything one needed to enjoy cycling. The manager was very helpful and supportive of what we were doing. When I told him that our riding was taking its toll on what the Army would call our "fourth point of contact," he offered a solution. The sheep-skin bicycle seat covers we purchased were a lifesaver. We rode the next 2,000 miles in comfort.

After some tough cycling, we made it to a refuge, the home of Walter and Cindy Wolff and their three children, Aaron, Jason, and Brandon. Walter was the brother of my friend Eddie Wolff. Eddie and Walter were wonderful people, the kind of men who would give you the shirts off their backs. Our stay with Walter and his family for a couple of days was a highlight of our trip. Walter contacted the Wichita morning newspaper, the *Wichita Eagle-Beacon*, and a reporter and photographer appeared to cover our story. As Berti and I were interviewed, the photographer clicked away, and Stephen really hammed it up. The next morning, our story and pictures appeared in the morning paper, and Walter and his family were more excited than we were. Walter brought home an armful of newspapers and passed them out to his neighbors.

We joined Walter and his family on a trip to the Sedgwick County Zoo. We had a great time, and it marked Stephen's first trip to a zoo, another milestone in his life. After the zoo, we participated in a weekly ritual for the Walter Wolff family. We all had large bowls of ice cream topped with strawberries and whipped cream. This is the "dessert of champions," as far as cyclists are concerned. Berti and I built up our depleted calorie count. Kansas had a way of stealing calories from cyclists foolish enough to bicycle across the state. Stephen had his share of ice cream too, even though he hadn't worked quite as hard as Berti and I had.

We had a going-away breakfast on Thursday morning, July 21st. Walter went all out preparing eggs, bacon, sausage, toast, and coffee. We continued to learn the lesson that our cross-country bicycle trip was not about the bikes, not about the scenery–it was about the people. There were many parallels between our bicycle trip across America and life itself. Understanding that good friends and family are the most precious things in our lives is a lesson we need to remember. In the end, you are judged by the people you positively impact, not by the money you make.

Chapter Thirteen

Lazy Louie

WE MET MANY RETIREES ON OUR LONG JOURNEY EAST,
sharing campfires with couples touring the country by motorcycle,
Vanagon, and recreational vehicle. Others took on the role of park
hosts at state parks for 30 days at a time. They may have been retired
from their jobs, but they were not retired from life. We met one
such man in the heart of the Ozark Mountains.

After our stay in Wichita, we were well-rested, and it felt good to
have the open road in front of us again. We left Wichita as local
celebrities due to the article about our trip which appeared in the
Wichita Eagle-Beacon. Outside of Wichita, after about 90 minutes
of cycling, we stopped for a rest. As we stretched our legs, a car
pulled over to the side of the road, and a short, plump gentleman
with a broad smile rolled down the window. He told us he had seen
our story and picture in the newspaper and wanted to wish us well.
Later we arrived in Fall River, and we had offers from three different people to spend the night with them. It was like a bidding
war. We chose to stay with Elsie Shinkle and her husband. They
had a huge, well-kept, recreational vehicle parked alongside their
home, and it provided comfortable quarters for the night.

As we cycled through eastern Kansas toward the Ozark Mountains
in Missouri, the hills were a roller-coaster ride of steep climbs and

equally steep descents. My health started to fail me. The tough climbs, the unrelenting heat, the weight I was pulling, and the stress associated with having the safety of our young son on my mind all began to create wear and tear on my body. Swollen glands and blisters formed inside my mouth. I took it in stride, never doubting we would complete my–now *our*–dream of cycling across the United States. We simply slowed the pace down and kept on pedaling.

The next day, our goal was to reach Pittsburg, Kansas. I was feeling much better during the day's ride. We camped in Pittsburg City Park. The night was very humid, and we slept on top of our sleeping bags rather than inside of them. It was not a good night's sleep for any of us. The next morning, I cooked up some oatmeal on our camping stove, and we headed east out of town.

Thirty-five miles later, we reached Golden City. The 35-mile trek was hot and humid. There were no services prior to reaching Golden City, though I did find a church where we were able to replenish our water supply. We arrived at the Golden City town park and were happy and surprised to find a public bathhouse, so the three of us took showers. Once refreshed, we found Cooky's Café. Berti enjoyed baked ham while I devoured fried chicken, topped off by pie and ice cream. Stephen ate half of Berti's dinner and dessert. Eating chow was always a team effort, just like everything else we did. We stayed in Golden City until 4:30 p.m., waiting for the hottest part of the day to pass. While cooling off in Golden City, we met two cross-country cyclists. Both had begun their journey in Seattle. One was heading to Philadelphia, Pennsylvania, and the other to South Carolina. Stephen stole the show again, and he became the subject of their photos.

As the sun began to lower in the western sky, we continued along Route 126 to the town of Greenfield and picked up Road U to Walnut Grove, Kansas. Walnut Grove not only had a quaint ring to it, but it reminded me of Mayberry, and I expected to see Andy Griffith walking down Main Street. Instead of meeting Andy, we met Richard and Alice Counts. They insisted that we spend the night with them. The Counts provided a comfortable place to sleep in their day room, and Alice cooked up turkey patty sandwiches for us. After a very hot day, we happily took a dip in Richard and Alice's swimming pool. Stephen swam like a fish. Stephen became worn out from the swimming, and coupled with the air conditioning, he slept soundly. I was glad we had a roof over our heads because it rained during the night. The timing of the Counts' invitation was perfect. Before leaving Walnut Grove, I phoned WARM radio and provided another progress report. More and more people in northeastern Pennsylvania were tuning in to the radio station to hear about our adventure. Social media was not in America's vocabulary in 1983, so our radio interviews captivated people.

At Marshfield, we crossed into Missouri and the heart of the Ozark Mountains on July 25th. As we cycled toward Hartville, Missouri, on Route 2, we arrived at Lazy Louie's Bicycle Camp. Louis Schultz was a retired machinist. In the mid-1970s, thousands of cyclists were traveling the TransAmerica Bicycle Trail that ran along Route 2 in front of Louie's rural homestead. His house was at a point along the route that caused cyclists to stop and ask if they could fill their water bottles. Louie was more than happy to help needy cyclists quench their thirst. After a time, Louie decided to build small shelters on his property so cyclists could camp and spend the night. Louie collected a modest payment from campers, but his real reward was the conversations he had and the stories he heard. This was how Lazy Louie's Bicycle Camp came to be. The camp was iconic. Cyclists spread the word about the camp through the cross-country cyclist grapevine. Berti and I heard about the camp hundreds of miles before entering Missouri, and we were looking forward to spending the night at this fixture along the TransAmerica Bicycle Trail.

Just as Berti and I had heard about Lazy Louie, he had heard about us. As cyclists passed us, headed in Louie's direction, they informed him that two parents and a baby were coming his way. In Louie's nine years of greeting cyclists, he had only one other baby stay at his camp. In 1982, two parents on a tandem bicycle stayed at Louie's with a 22-month-old boy. Stephen holds the record for the youngest adventurer to stay at Lazy Louie's camp. When we arrived at the camp, Louie was waiting for us. He stood along the roadside, an elderly man with thick black-framed glasses, about six feet tall, dressed in blue work pants, a blue-and-white flannel shirt, and a blue baseball cap with just the right amount of sweat and dirt on it to telegraph that he was still a working man. Louie was a self-proclaimed "good ole boy." Louie told us he normally did not keep milk in his house. However, with our expected arrival, he had made a special trip to the grocery store, and he had a cold pitcher of whole milk waiting for Stephen. Louie also gave us fresh apples from his tree. Berti and I were grateful.

Louie took to Stephen as a grandfather would. He cradled Stephen in his arms and gave him a tour of the camp. Later in the evening, Louie played his guitar and sang songs he had written, crooning about the travelers he had met as they passed through his camp. Louie did have a bit of entrepreneurship in his blood, and he marketed cassette tapes of the songs he recorded for $6 each. Louie predicted rain for the evening and offered to let us bed down in one of his shelters rather than deal with a wet tent the next morning. I thanked him and accepted his offer.

The three of us slept like rocks in the comfort of Lazy Louie's Bicycle Camp. We awoke around 7 a.m., and Louie had fresh coffee brewing for Berti and me and, of course, fresh cold milk for Stephen. After breakfast, Berti, Stephen, and I were on the road again, happy for having met a TransAmerica Bicycle Trail legend, never realizing that Louie felt the same way about us. On November 15, 1983, three months after Berti, Stephen, and I completed the ride of our lives and fulfilled our dream, a cassette tape and a letter arrived from Lazy Louie. The last line in his letter read, "It was one of the highlights of the year to have you nice folks stay at the LL camp. God bless."

Chapter Fourteen

TO THE OZARKS AND BEYOND

THE HILLS OF THE OZARKS WERE UNRELENTING. THE
Ozark Mountains were much tougher on us than the Rockies. At
least the Rockies were a steady grade. The Ozarks took on the pat-
tern of high-frequency sound waves. They were not the tallest hills
we climbed, but they were the steepest hills we faced, and they kept
coming at us, one after another.

The steep grades took their toll on my bike due to the heavy weight I
was lugging. I inspected the bicycles daily. One morning I detected
a crack in my chain. I stopped at the next bicycle shop we came to
and replaced the worn chain. I was nervous the whole time getting
there, hoping the chain would not give way when I stood on my
pedals cranking up a steep hill. I knew that if that chain broke, I
would be singing soprano.

It was around this time when I almost lost it one morning. We
awoke in a town park to a very hot and humid sunrise. During the
night, Stephen's diaper had leaked, and the smell of urine on our
sleeping bags was stifling. I flew into a rage and ripped the sleeping
bags out of the tent and threw them to the ground. I took my anger
out on Berti and scolded her without justification. I was screaming
that we had to find a laundromat before we biked another mile.
Berti was wiser than I was. She refused to accept the invitation to

the fight I was offering. She calmly packed the sleeping bags and promised we would find a washer and dryer before nightfall. Berti knew how to calm me down, and I was lucky to have such a good partner in my life.

We cycled into Houston, Texas County. I had to look at our map and make sure we were still in Missouri rather than Texas. I confirmed we had not strayed into the Lone Star State as the name of the town suggested. We decided to camp at Emmett Kelly Park. I fried some ham-and-cheese patties on our one-burner stove, and they tasted pretty good. I was becoming quite a chef. We continued to meet fellow cyclists. Two college students from Pittsburgh, Pennsylvania, were sharing the park with us. They were cycling across the United States and raising money for a Christian foundation named Habitat. Just as we were raising money for the Boys Club of Scranton, these two cyclists were also riding with a purpose.

As we cycled from Houston the next morning, the scenery was sensational, and we faced one of our most difficult days of cycling. At Alley Springs, we encountered some very steep hills. The going was tough, but we were able to climb every hill. We never had to walk our bikes. We ended the day at Owls Bend Campground. We had cycled 60 miles during the day over some very difficult terrain. We awoke at Owls Bend on July 28th, and I cooked oatmeal over an open campfire and mixed in apples for good measure. A family camping next to us visited our campsite and took pictures of Stephen climbing into his bicycle trailer as we were getting ready to start the day.

The hills seemed to get steeper as the days wore on. Either the hills were getting steeper, or we were getting weaker. With the hot weather and the terrain, we burned calories at a record pace. Traveling east on Route 106 into Ellington, we rested long enough to have a couple of Twinkies and some chocolate milk. In 1983, Twinkies were the traditional energy food of cross-country cyclists. The first commercially released energy bars did not appear until 1986. Berti and I tried our best to select healthy food for our diet, but some days we had to succumb to comfort food. On hot days when the hills challenged our legs, consuming a pound cake and a quart of ice cream topped off with strawberries was a great reward.

We left Ellington on Route 21 North, cycling through hot and hilly woodlands. The sun fried the road in front of us, and I thought for a moment that it had fried my brain. I thought I was hallucinating. In the road ahead, I saw an image I had a hard time making sense of. As Berti and I came to a stop at the bottom of a steep hill, we saw three men coming toward us. Two were naked except for Speedos and roller skates. The third man was on a touring bicycle loaded down with stuffed panniers. They were Frenchmen, all brothers. Two were roller-skating across the United States. The third brother was carrying provisions for the three of them on his bicycle. They had begun their journey in Virginia, and their destination was California. We were amazed at what they were attempting, and they were just as amazed by us. Their cameras came out, and they took plenty of pictures of Stephen, Berti, and me. We took the time to share stories of our journey. It was a nice break from climbing the steep hills. Every day brought amazing surprises.

We reached Centerville around noon and had lunch at the court-house square, waiting until about 4 p.m. to mount our bicycles again in order to escape the hottest part of the day. Our reward at the end of the hard day's cycling was Johnson's Shut-Ins State Park. We took a dip in the river that ran through the park, and the cool water refreshed our bodies and souls. Then we treated ourselves to a hot shower. The difficult cycling of the last few days helped us to once again appreciate the simple things in life. We would not enjoy the earth's blessings as much if we did not encounter challenges along the way.

We continued our adventure across Missouri, cycling into the towns of Pilot Knob, Doe Run, and Farmington. In Farmington, the sky opened, and cats and dogs fell from the clouds. We took refuge under the roof of a supermarket. Customers were treated to a weird sight as they entered the store; a bearded guy in tight shorts accompanied by a lovely young lady and a beautiful baby. The hard rain continued all afternoon. It was the kind of rain we did not want to start out in. I decided to go down the street to Saint Joseph's Catholic Church. I could see the steeple clearly from our perch in front of the supermarket. I asked the priest for a dry place to spend the night. He sent us to the Friendly Motel and picked up the $14 tab for the night's stay. It was a fleabag motel, but at least it was dry.

We awoke at the Friendly Motel on the morning of July 31st. I checked myself and my family for fleas, and all appeared to be okay. Berti and I reflected on our trek through Missouri over a cup of coffee before we began our day of cycling. We agreed that Lazy Louie was a special person. This retired machinist who looked the part of a tough blue-collar worker had a soft heart. He was an example of how helping others leads to a happy life. We also agreed that the three brothers from France, two of whom were roller-skating across the United States, were the most amazing group of cross-country travelers we had come across. We had no doubt they would finish their journey to the West Coast, and we were sure they would experience the same warm reception from the average American as we had.

We were grateful to the Catholic priest who lodged us in the dry comfort of the Friendly Motel, and we bade him farewell before making our way toward the Mississippi River and the Illinois state line. We traveled on a series of roads and then crossed a bridge over the Mississippi River into Chester, Illinois. Crossing the Mississippi River was a milestone. We knew there was no stopping us now. The Ozarks had been a challenge, but along with the tough terrain, we were treated to beautiful scenery and neighborly people. We had only a few more states to go. Illinois, Kentucky, Ohio, and Pennsylvania awaited us. We had been to the Ozarks, and now we were set to travel beyond.

Chapter Fifteen

School Days

AS WE ROLLED ACROSS THE UNITED STATES, WE GAINED
quite an education. This adventure had taken us back to school in
a way. We learned lessons every day as we shared our time with
principals and students, coaches and players, in schools and colleges,
quads and lawns. We were schooled by strangers in small towns and
campgrounds. The curriculum was life changing.

We rolled onto the bridge crossing the Mississippi River and came
to a stop. We looked down at Ol' Man River and took in the muddy
view. It was fabulous. I realized many people from my hometown
in northeastern Pennsylvania had never been as far west as the
Mississippi River, and I felt very fortunate for the experiences this
cross-country adventure provided to me and my family.

From Chester, Illinois, we cycled south on Route 3 and then rode
east. Then we turned onto Route 149, a narrow and congested route.
We were happy to arrive at Murphysboro State Park. The deciduous
trees on the hills surrounding Murphysboro Lake reflected off the
water in the bright afternoon sun. The air was fresh, and the lake
was cool. This was a welcome respite from the narrow road we had
just negotiated under the burning sun. We enjoyed a relaxing afternoon hiking along the shore of the lake. We met a fisherman who
had three bluegills on his stringer. He told us that Murphysboro

Lake was home to some of the best fishing in the state. The next morning, we learned that Murphysboro was also home to a gang of bandits.

Raccoons are thieves. We learned that the hard way at Murphysboro Lake. I got lazy and did not stow away the provisions we planned to have for breakfast. I awoke and got ready to stoke the stove when I noticed the oatmeal I planned to cook had been ravaged. Upon further inspection, I found that our biscuits were reduced to crumbs. Tiny paw prints informed me that we had nighttime visitors who were as hungry as we were. They had beaten us to the punch. Our breakfast would have to wait until later that morning. We broke camp and began our day's ride on empty stomachs. We were cycling on fumes.

We rode into Carbondale, Illinois. This was a good town to stock up on provisions. The bicycle shop was well supplied, and I took care of some preventive maintenance. It was always a treat for me to stop at these small-town bicycle shops. The shop employees were cool. Most were into bicycle touring or bicycle racing. You do not find many out-of-shape people working in a bike shop. You usually do not find many rich people working there either. Working at a bike shop has many benefits, but high wages is not one of them. The bicycle shop staff were also very informative. We would hear stories about other cross-country cyclists who had passed through. We could acquire good intelligence about road conditions ahead. Fellow cyclists are the best source of information on what route to take. Since they cycle the roads themselves, they become sensitive to road surfaces and grades and provide accurate information.

Carbondale was the home of Southern Illinois University (SIU). In the research I had done prior to our bicycle tour, I read that during the summer, many college campuses offer a haven for cross-country cyclists. Usually, in the summer, there were not many students on campus, and with the right amount of luck, a cross-country cyclist might be able to score a free dorm room for the night.

I reflected on my days at college. I had attended a Jesuit university. The University of Scranton was originally founded as Saint
Thomas College. At one time, it was an all-boys school. By the
time I attended school there, it was coed, which did not help with
my concentration during long history lectures. The University of
Scranton did not have a traditional campus. The college classroom
buildings were intermingled with the busy streets and businesses
of the city. Today that look has changed. It began to look more like
a campus as the business acumen and treasures of the Jesuit community were used to purchase property and improve the aesthetics.

My own experience at college was not traditional. I commuted from
home, and since I worked in my father's family business, I logged
in more hours working than I did studying. This accounted for my
low GPA as an undergraduate, but at least I escaped with a piece of
sheepskin claiming I had a Bachelor of Science degree. Years later,
when I worked on my MBA, I did much better. To this day, I still
have recurring nightmares about college as an undergrad, dreaming
that the school year is ending and there is a course or two I forgot to
attend, leading to failing grades and preventing me from obtaining
that precious diploma.

My most enjoyable time at the University of Scranton, also known
as "Da U," was the Reserve Officer Training Corps (ROTC) program. The ROTC cadre trained me on how to be an officer and a
gentleman, and my fellow ROTC cadets became my best friends.
The day I graduated from college was also the day I swore an oath to
"support and defend the Constitution of the United States, against
all enemies, foreign and domestic." I was proud to be a commissioned officer in the United States Army, and I was looking forward
to beginning my tour on active duty.

As I thought back to my college experience, I decided that SIU
would probably be a cool place to stay. We cycled onto the campus
and started to nose around. We were directed to the Alpha Tau
Omega fraternity house. This place was not an animal house. It was
upscale. Alpha Tau Omega is America's leadership fraternity. Their

tagline is "helping college men develop their ability to be effective leaders for a lifetime." This was exactly the kind of frat house a guy like me would want his wife and son to bed down in for the night. We were not disappointed. The students treated us like rock stars. It also did not hurt that our room was air-conditioned. A reporter from the campus newspaper, the *Daily Egyptian*, interviewed us and took pictures. The newspaper staff was efficient. By the next morning, our picture and a short story appeared in the early edition. The only negative thing that happened was they spelled our names wrong, but we got over it quickly.

As we cycled the next day, I noticed my rear wheel had come out of true and had begun to rub against my rear brake pad. I stopped and found that a spoke in the rear wheel had broken. I was able to replace the spoke without too much trouble and tightened the spoke nipple enough to get the wheel straight. When cycling long distances, these mechanical issues are not unusual. The weight, the road surfaces, and the hills work in collusion against the engineering marvel known as the humble bicycle. A little common sense and mechanical aptitude go a long way in salvaging a cross-country bicycle excursion.

A few miles later, Berti had a flat tire which I quickly repaired. We had our share of flat tires during our trip. One of the most common road hazards when traversing the United States is thorns. The glass from broken bottles is another source of frustration for cyclists, especially in large cities. When these mechanical dilemmas present themselves, they are best met with a positive attitude. It is all about placing things in the proper perspective. A bad day on a bicycle is better than a good day behind a desk.

On August 2nd we followed rural roads until we arrived at Dixon Springs State Park while there was still enough daylight to enjoy the surroundings. The park resides in the Shawnee Hills and is surrounded by giant rocks. Water flows through the rock formations, providing tubs to lounge in. Hiking trails twist through an interesting maze of elephant-sized rocks, and ferns and tall trees surround the footpaths. We were only charged $1 to camp for the night. Even without showers in the camp, that price was a bargain.

Before dark, a family camping nearby came to visit our campsite. They invited us to use their camper trailer to take a shower, and we gladly accepted. There was no limit to the wonderful people we were meeting. After we freshened up, our campsite neighbors came over to visit us again. They were excited to hear about where we had been and where we were off to. They were amazed at Stephen's happy demeanor and how well he was holding up after living out of bicycle panniers and a trailer for over two months. Stephen was a hardy soul, but he had his challenges along the way too. We had caused him an upset stomach by feeding him spoiled powdered milk a month earlier. He also cut two back teeth while on this adventure. That is something I was glad I didn't have to do.

We awoke as the sun began to rise over Dixon Springs State Park. From Dixon Springs, we traveled on a series of low-traffic back roads. The sun was bright, the trees were green, and a slight breeze blew at our backs. Our wheels hummed as we glided along the roadway. We arrived at the banks of the Ohio River and traveled across the river by ferry to Cave-In-Rock, Illinois. We chalked up another state and were now in Kentucky

Cycling through the Bluegrass State, we sailed past farms and pastures. Berti and I would spot sheep and bleat "baa" at them as we cycled by. They would simply stare and would not answer us. We passed horse farms with brown stallions grazing in the green-blue grass. We cycled in forests of maple trees draping the road that we followed in comforting shade.

Our day ended in Clay, Kentucky. As we surveyed the town, we assessed our best place to camp was behind the local high school. We made a great decision. The school principal saw us wheeling our bicycles behind the school and came to visit us. As soon as he saw Stephen, he took an immediate liking to our trio. He opened the school gym so we could use the showers and kept the door unlocked all night, so the restrooms were accessible. We were very appreciative and amazed at his kindness. The hospitality of the residents of Clay continued as a lady stopped by to say hello, bringing along a peach pie she had just baked. The thoughtfulness of this community was heartening.

We left Clay in the morning with a very good taste in our mouths, not only from the hospitality but also from that fresh peach pie. We cycled through the town of Dixon, staying on the TransAmerica Bicycle Trail, and we finished our day in Whitesville. It was a day of cycling along rural roads bordered by green pastures and babbling creeks, with very little traffic to contend with.

In Whitesville, we stopped alongside Mary of the Woods Catholic Church. I asked the priest for permission to camp on the church grounds. Permission was granted, but we were disappointed that we were not invited to take a shower, especially since the church had a high school complete with a gym. I guess the Clay High School principal had spoiled us.

The night spent in our tent behind the church was miserable. It was a hot August night, which made for restless sleep. I was glad when the morning came, and I could crawl out of the tent. We treated ourselves to a cereal-and-milk breakfast and then went out on the open road again. We only biked 35 miles. After a rough sleep the night before, we wanted to give ourselves a break. Berti also wanted time to do some laundry. Our riding ended at Rough River State Park. They called this place a "resort," and it had earned that name. It really was a resort, offering golf, tennis, swimming, and a large recreational lodge. They had everything. There are many hidden gems in the forest.

The next gem we found was My Old Kentucky Home State Park in Bardstown. We set up camp near the playground, which Stephen approved of. The showers felt good after another hot day of cycling. I made some soup for dinner, and it tasted as good as ever. At the time, I didn't realize we were in bourbon country. In 1983, I was in my 20's and had not explored the pleasures of John Barleycorn beyond the taste of beer.

Our next stop in Kentucky was the state capital of Frankfort which we reached on August 7th. Since we had good luck at Southern Illinois University, we thought we would visit Kentucky State University (KSU). We ventured onto the campus, and it was like a ghost town. We had a hard time finding anyone. Finally, we met a man with either big thighs or tight shorts. He also wore a golf shirt and a baseball cap, and a whistle on a lanyard hung from around his neck. He introduced himself as an assistant football coach. He told us the football team reported early, prior to the fall semester, so that they could practice double sessions. He offered to put us up in the dormitory with the college football team. Success! This sounded good to us. At least I thought it was a good deal, and I was excited to be spending the night with the football team.

Once we entered the dorm, Berti was not very excited about it. As we were led to our room on the second floor of the dormitory, Berti had to squeeze past sweaty 350-pound linemen moving up and down the stairwell in jockey shorts. The KSU football team went by the name of Thorobreds, and I could see why. Every football player I encountered was as big as a horse. Throughout the evening, Berti had to shuttle herself in and out of the men's bathroom, taking a shower and using the other facilities while the team was eating or at meetings. Stephen and I had to stand guard at the men's room door while Berti did her business. I thought this was comical, but Berti wasn't laughing.

Our dorm room was not spacious. There were two single beds that were more the size of cots than beds. I wasn't quite sure how these huge football players were able to fit on beds that were better designed for an eighth-grader than a college athlete. However, Berti and I made do. Berti and Stephen slept in one bed, and I slept in the other. During the night, a football player mistakenly entered our room. This accounted for a rude awakening, but the football player was apologetic and left our room without a fuss.

Once this happened, Berti made me push the chest of drawers against the door since our room did not have a lock on the door. I slept peacefully the rest of the night, but I don't think Berti slept as well as I did.

We awoke early the next morning. Stephen and I posted ourselves on guard duty outside of the men's restroom again in order to ensure Berti had privacy for her morning constitutional. Then we got off to an early start on our bicycles. Berti wanted to be on her way before she was forced to maneuver around the offensive line. To Berti's chagrin, the football players were also early risers, so she had another close encounter with these college athletes who were two to three times my size. Berti was a bit disgruntled as we left the campus, but this episode has provided Berti, Stephen, and me with many laughs over the years as we reminisced about our stay with the KSU Thorobreds.

Chapter Sixteen

A Horse of a Different Color

THE KENTUCKY STATE UNIVERSITY OFFENSIVE LINEMEN
were as big as horses, and our stay at KSU was not the last time
we would encounter horses in Kentucky. As we cycled alongside
green pastures lined with white fences, horses would see us gliding
by and run alongside us. These horses were magnificent animals,
their muscles glistening in the Kentucky sunshine.

We bade farewell to the KSU football players, who watched us
cycle off with curious expressions on their faces. They probably
were trying to figure out how a thin guy like me could pull so much
weight behind his bicycle. We made a pit stop at Granny's Kitchen
before leaving Frankfort. Just as the name implied, the breakfast
was just like home cooking, and the waitress serving us looked like
a grandmother. Once well-fed, we tackled some more hills as we
rode along the scenic Routes 460, 62, and 27 into Falmouth. In
Falmouth, we met more horses.

We had a connection in Falmouth. Diane Walsh was a distant
relative, and my sister Ruth connected us through a phone call
as Berti, Stephen, and I traveled cross-country. Diane and her
husband David were thrilled to invite us into their home. David

was an MD, and he had a medical practice in Falmouth. David and Diane were true animal lovers. David probably should have become a veterinarian. The Walshes raised show horses, and their favorite breed was the Morgan. Morgan horses have shiny dark skin and flowing manes. They also have a rich history, dating back to the nineteenth century. Union General Philip Sheridan's horse, Winchester, was said to be a Morgan. According to the National Museum of American History Behring Center, Sheridan renamed his steed from its original name of Rienzi following his famous ride from Winchester, Virginia, to Cedar Creek, Virginia on October 19, 1864. Astride his horse at Cedar Creek, Sheridan rallied his troops and turned almost certain defeat into victory. Most cavalrymen, both from the Union and the Confederacy, rode Morgan horses.

When Berti had worked on the family farm in Austria, she plucked chickens, mucked stalls, butchered pigs, drove tractors, and milked cows the old-fashioned way. However, her farm did not have horses. The only farm animals Berti had ever ridden were cows and occasionally an oversized hog. When Berti saw David and Diane's Morgan horses, she wanted to try horseback riding, something she had always wanted to do. If my dream was cycling cross-country, Berti's dream was to ride a horse. In Falmouth, her dream was realized. The Walshes saddled up one of their gentlest horses, and Berti was up on the horse in no time. She even gave Stephen a ride around the corral. This was a landmark moment for Berti and Stephen as the horse strutted along bearing two novice riders.

If David had a second love after horses, it was for music. David made his own Appalachian dulcimers. I had never heard of a dulcimer, but David schooled me on the instrument. An Appalachian dulcimer is a stringed instrument with usually four strings. The dulcimer lies on the lap while the musician plucks and frets. David was a poor man's musician. He loved to compose his own words, and during our visit, he crooned songs about the hills, valleys, and of course the horses of Kentucky. It was fun to listen to David sing his homespun songs, but I must admit, if he had recorded cassette tapes, I would not have bought one. Some music is better in person.

The Walshes lived on a spread complete with a two-story house trimmed with blue shutters and featuring a large wraparound front porch. The front-porch swing chirped a rhythmic tune as it rocked back and forth. The horses grazed in a large pasture and drank from a spring-fed pond. Shade trees provided comfort for the horses when they tired of the Kentucky sun. The stables in the barn were well kept and lined with fresh straw. It was truly a hotel for horses. The farm was perfect for raising these award-winning animals.

The evening with David and Diane was as relaxing as the afternoon was fun. Diane prepared chicken, potatoes, broccoli, and a fresh salad, along with oven-fresh biscuits. These home-cooked meals were a treasure for Berti, Stephen, and me. Fueling up at these safe havens, along with the dinner conversations, nourished our bodies and livened our spirits. Stephen was meeting many people with big hearts at an early age.

We continued to make news while in Falmouth. The editor of the local paper visited the Walsh farm himself. He snapped pictures, with Stephen and his trailer as the centerpiece of the photos. According to the editor's newspaper article, Berti, Stephen and I had been receiving national coverage from newspapers, television, and radio. Stephen was a child celebrity, and he wasn't even 18 months old.

We enjoyed our stay at the Walsh farm so much that we did not say our good-byes and get back on the road again until 11 a.m. on August 9th. The horseback riding, the home-cooked meal, and the serenade David provided while strumming his dulcimer were all memorable events.

Every day we met people who added to the depth and breadth of our adventurous ride across America. As we traveled across the United States, we were offered meals and invitations to spend the night from countless strangers. We developed a "spider-sense" when deciding who to accept invitations from. Spider-sense is a heightened sense of awareness to detect danger before it develops and an awareness of who one can trust. Another term for spider-sense is "street smart". The longer one travels the road, the more attuned that person becomes to the character of others. It is much like learning who to befriend as we go through life. Making decisions about whom to associate with sets the tone for the life one leads.

Deciding who to hang out with is an important skill, and the quicker we learn that the greater the chance we will live a wholesome and successful life. There is a great deal of truth to Proverbs 27:17. It reads, "As iron sharpens iron, so one person sharpens another." The verse speaks of teamwork, resiliency, and how associating with virtuous people makes you stronger. If you want to fly with eagles, don't hang out with turkeys. This is especially important for adolescents to figure out at a young age. That does not mean you should not try to help other people who are not as talented as you or who are struggling. But it does mean that you should not allow unethical or unprincipled people to drag you down.

As Berti, Stephen, and I continued our adventure, we were growing stronger as a family. Similarly, I suspected that many of the people we met on our journey were strengthened by our story and what we were accomplishing. Likewise, we met many wonderful people, and we were strengthened by their stories and how they were living their lives.

Chapter Seventeen

OHIO STATE

BEING FROM PENNSYLVANIA, I WAS NATURALLY A PENN
State fan. After our journey through the "Buckeye State", I still
didn't root for Ohio State, but I did become a fan of the state of Ohio.

We cycled through Maysville, Kentucky, a town dotted with church
steeples and buildings from a bygone era. The Ohio River moved
slowly past this slow-moving, historic town. Daniel Boone was
one of Maysville's founders. We crossed the Ohio River by way of
the Simon Kenton Memorial Bridge, which connects Maysville,
Kentucky with Aberdeen, Ohio. Simon Kenton was a frontiersman,
born in the eighteenth century, and a friend of Daniel Boone. The
bridge was adorned with suspension cables and tall towers. The
1,060-foot span bowed upward, and we felt as though we were
climbing a hill again as we pedaled toward the center of the bridge
and gazed at the Ohio River flowing beneath us. The people of this
region either lived in the past or had a fine appreciation for history,
naming a bridge built in 1931 for a settler born in 1755.

As we arrived on the eastern side of the Ohio River, our next stop
was Aberdeen, Ohio. Aberdeen was only one-tenth of the size
of Maysville, with a population of under 1,000, but it also had a
storied history. The town sat astride a frontier road through the
northwest territory known as Zane's Trace, which followed Native

American trails through the region. We found a safe place to camp behind the Aberdeen Methodist Church.

We were on the road the next morning, August 10th, by 9:30 a.m. We headed east on Route 52, following the Ohio River. The natural beauty of the route lulled me into a meditative state of mind. I was aroused by a distinct pinging sound and then I felt my rear wheel dragging against my brake pad. Spokes on my rear wheel began to snap, one after the other, about every 10 miles. This problem slowed our progress. The elbow of a spoke is the area that hugs the hole of the hub of the wheel and is the weakest part of a spoke. That was the area of the spokes that began to fail. The weight I was pulling was a lot for my rear wheel to handle. I stopped to replace the snapped spokes and knew I would have to find a good bicycle shop soon and have my rear wheel rebuilt. To this point, we had cycled well over 3,000 miles.

We found a private campground a few miles west of Portsmouth, Ohio. Shawnee Campground rested alongside the Ohio River. The leaves of the oak trees acted as giant fans as the breeze blew through the campsite. I slept like a log. In the morning we treated ourselves to a hearty breakfast prepared on our Peak 1 one-burner camping stove. We were getting a lot of mileage out of that single burner. We cycled into Portsmouth and I found a small bicycle shop where I was able to score some spokes in order to replenish others that I predicted would snap throughout the course of the day. Unfortunately, my prediction was correct.

As the day wore on, the skies became threatening and dark clouds hovered overhead. The sky finally opened and drenched Berti and me as we continued to head east. Stephen stayed dry and warm in his trailer and probably wondered why we were so anxious to find a location to end our cycling for the day. We found a Holiday Inn along the roadside and sprinted for cover under the roof above the entrance to the hotel. We were happy to find this dry refuge. About this time, marble-sized hailstones began falling from the sky. The hail was denting the cars in the parking lot. I could only imagine the damage it would have done to two thin-skinned cyclists trapped in the melee.

I waddled into the hotel lobby, leaving puddles of water in my wake. I tried to talk my way into getting a complimentary room for the evening, but I was not able to sell the manager on that idea. However, I was able to wrangle an employee discount, and for the sum of $21, we had a dry room for the evening. Just as importantly, it gave us the opportunity to dry our clothes. Weight is a key consideration when cycling cross-country, which meant we carried a minimal amount of clothing.

The morning of August 12th brought dry skies. After spending the evening at the Holiday Inn, we were also dry. We bade farewell to the Holiday Inn and logged in about 60 miles before we reached the town of Circleville, Ohio. We were within spitting distance of Ohio State University, if we had been driving in a car. However, Ohio State was 25 miles away, a significant distance for our weary legs. We decided to spend the night in Circleville. Circleville was famous for the Circleville Pumpkin Show, billed as the "greatest free show on earth." Even though the festival was still two months away, flyers advertising the Pumpkin Show adorned every telephone pole on Main street. As we explored Circleville, we determined the best place to pitch our tent was behind the Circleville Presbyterian Church.

Our sleep behind the church was sound. After we woke the next morning, a fireman at the firehouse next door to the church waved us over. We had a conversation about a recent fire he had to fight that involved him rescuing a young child. After we listened to his inspiring tale, he treated us to a hot cup of coffee.

A young newspaper reporter from the *Herald*, Marty Minor, saw our caravan at the firehouse and hustled over our way. He took pictures and asked a flurry of questions about where we had traveled from, where we were going, and what the toughest part of our trip had been. I told Marty the toughest part of our trip had been

Kansas, where we faced high winds and scorching temperatures. I added that the Ozark Mountains, with their steep climbs, had also been a challenge. He asked how much money the trip had cost us after being on the road for over two months. I estimated we had spent about $2,000, and most of the cost was keeping Stephen in clean diapers. As Berti and I spoke to Marty, we noted that we had logged approximately 3,600 miles and still had hundreds of miles to go until our journey ended in northeastern Pennsylvania. We were road warriors.

Marty also noted how unusual it was to cycle cross-country with a toddler. Berti and I were fortunate to spend so much time with our 17-month-old son. Stephen would sleep between Berti and me in the evening once we crawled inside our tent. He would wake with us and was all hands and feet as he helped me prepare breakfast in the morning. He seemed very comfortable in the nylon seat inside his bicycle trailer, and Berti and Stephen would talk and sing as we made our way along the TransAmerica Bicycle Trail. They could have eye contact since Stephen sat facing the rear of the trailer. The thin mosquito netting on the back of the trailer kept insects out, toys in, and Berti's eyes on Stephen. We enjoyed our time together during the day when we found a rest area along the side of the road, and Berti and I would log some playtime with Stephen. Berti and I did not require childcare for Stephen as we worked our eight-hour shifts cycling along the roadways.

We left Circleville around 10 a.m. after enjoyable conversations with the firemen from the Circleville Fire Company and the reporter from the *Herald*, Circleville's largest and probably only newspaper. We were on our way to Lancaster, Ohio, when a couple pulled their car over to the side of the road and stopped us. The lady in the passenger seat had graying hair and twinkling eyes. The driver, a large man with a balding head, also wore a large smile. It appeared they had read about us in one of the small-town newspapers. They invited us to have lunch with them at their home. They wanted to talk and hear about some of our experiences on the road. They were warm and genuine, and we readily accepted their offer.

Their home was down the road just a few miles and not out of our way, so this was an easy decision for us. We were treated to a home-cooked meal of pork chops and corn on the cob. Corn on the cob was one of Stephen's favorites.

The weather made us sweat, even when standing in the shade, and equally warm people kept appearing. Near the end of a hot summer's day in Ohio, we came upon a Protestant church and decided it would provide a good overnight rest stop. I approached a young man near the church and asked if he knew where the minister might be. The man held out his hand, shook mine, and introduced himself as the reverend. I asked permission to camp behind the church and was crestfallen, at least momentarily. His answer was a resounding, "No." He then stated that the weather was too hot and humid for us to stay outside. Instead, he opened the basement of the church to us. It was air conditioned. There were other attributes too. The floor had thick carpeting that we could lay our sleeping bags on. There were also restroom facilities and a shower. The basement had a complete kitchen that the minister made available to us. This man of God was a godsend.

Our next stop was Zanesville, Ohio. Berti and I both got strange vibes from the town. I cannot explain why, and I just chalked it up to a feeling we had. I mean no disrespect to Zanesville. It might be the nicest city in the world for all I know, but we had learned to trust our spider-sense, so we were extra careful and wanted to keep a low profile. It was late in the day when we arrived in Zanesville, and we had no choice but to stay there. We found a Catholic church, and the priest gave us permission to pitch our tent behind the church. There were not many amenities. The priest opened a restroom for us and gave us enough time to use the facilities and fill up our water bottles, but then he turned the key in the latch and locked it up again. We were happy at least to have a place to stay where we felt relatively safe. The priest did tell us he would keep a lookout for us throughout the night. He also offered a prayer for our safety. We were good to go.

We cycled out of Zanesville early the next morning, anxious to get on the road and log some more mileage. We negotiated suburban neighborhoods. There were cars parked along the curbside, and now and then we had to dodge driver-side car doors opening in our path. When these drivers exiting their cars saw us, many were apologetic, but I would have preferred if they had given a glance before thrusting their doors into the path of our bicycles. There were several intersections that we cycled through cautiously as cars impatiently halted at stop signs.

Then a near-tragedy occurred. Out of the corner of my eye, I saw a large German shepherd half-breed darting off a front porch. My contraption probably intimidated the dog, so the animal let me pass and went for Berti. The dog came at her at a dead sprint and leaped into the air, hitting Berti below shoulder level. This was a picture-perfect tackle, just the way I was taught at the Pine Forest football camp in the Pocono Mountains when I was 14 years old. Berti hit the paved road with a thump, and her head bounced after the initial thud. I jammed on my brakes and hopped off my bicycle. I was ready to fight the dog to the death if necessary, even though the animal outweighed me by about 20 pounds. The dog's master was immediately out on the street and contained the dog before more damage could be done. Berti was scraped up, had a dent in her helmet, and was startled. I checked out Berti and found no teeth marks. No need for the rabies protocol. Good news there. The bad news was that Berti had whacked her head hard on the road. I took her by the arm and guided her to the curb, where she took a seat. Berti seemed disoriented and I was worried, thinking my wife might be seriously injured.

Berti was spunky. Let's face it, she had to be spunky to agree to do this trip with me in the first place. After a few minutes, Berti regained her composure and was ready to go. I made her touch her finger to her nose and walk backward heel to toe just to be sure she had her faculties. More good news. Berti shook off the effects of the dog attack and was fine. It was hot and humid too. I guess you could say it was a dog-day afternoon.

We biked along Routes 40 and 22 to Salt Fork State Park. Salt Fork State Park is the largest state park in Ohio at more than 17,000 acres. The site where we camped provided a clear view of Salt Fork Lake. Gary and Susan Maupin happened to be our campground neighbors. They immediately opened their hearts to us. I think Stephen had something to do with it. The Maupins had a baby girl about the same age as Stephen. Her name was Penny, and Penny and Stephen became fast friends. Gary and Susan invited us to share a delicious chicken dinner with them. It was pleasant to have dinner with our new neighbors and not have to worry about preparing a seven-course meal on a one-burner camp stove.

I took on a Forrest Gump look during our cross-country travels. My hair grew long and unruly. Between the bicycle helmet I wore and the lack of a daily hot shower, there was not a lot I could do with my flowing locks. I also had a scraggly beard that I am sure scared some people. Berti, on the other hand, looked great. The time on the road bronzed her silky skin, and she was trim and fit. Stephen was holding up well. He experienced hundreds of playgrounds during our time on the road, so he was staying fit. Stephen was in good shape, was eating well, had plenty of love, and was as cute as ever. And now, at Salt Fork State Park, he found a friend to play with.

Chapter Eighteen

A Stitch in Time

BENJAMIN FRANKLIN WAS A GREAT PHILOSOPHER.
After over 200 years of our nation's history, he is probably still the
most quoted genius of all time. "A stitch in time saves nine" always
seems to ring true. Preventive maintenance is critical when engaged
in an excursion such as the cross-country journey we were conducting. There comes a time, though, when all the preventive maintenance in the world cannot prevent the inevitable from occurring.
I would have to find a shop that could rebuild the rear wheel on
my bicycle.

As we prepared to break camp at Salt Fork State Park on August
15th, Stephen was heartbroken, having to say good-bye to his new
friend, Penny. After leaving the park, we expected smooth sailing.
Not so fast—three very steep hills stood in our way as we left the
serenity of Salt Fork and the good wishes of the Maupins. We followed Road 21 north, and over the course of 60 miles of rural roads,
we reached Carrollton, Ohio. The town was named for local resident Charles Carroll, the last surviving signer of the Declaration of
Independence. The courthouse was a majestic multistory greystone
building, and it kept watch over the rest of the town.

I had a very difficult decision to make. Canton, Ohio, was about
25 miles to the northwest. I had been a longtime pro football fan.

I was a loyal fan of the Green Bay Packers, especially the Packers of the Lombardi era. I knew the Hall of Fame in Canton already had many of Lombardi's Packers enshrined. It would be a highlight for me to visit the renowned facility. However, reality set in. At this point in our journey, Berti and I decided Canton would be a bit too far out of our way. We also tended to place Stephen first. We didn't think Stephen would enjoy the museum atmosphere of the Hall of Fame at his tender age. Since we planned to live in Pennsylvania, we felt Canton would be close enough for us to visit at some time in the future.

After scouting around Carrollton, we could not find a nest that would be suitable for the evening. We saw a sign identifying a nearby fairgrounds and decided to bike that way and conduct reconnaissance. It was the perfect location for a one-night stand—plenty of buildings, a grandstand, and easy access to enter the facility. We felt comfortable with what we saw. We decided to stay at the county fairgrounds. I pitched our forest-green backpacking tent behind the blue-ribbon watermelon pavilion, and we settled down for the evening.

Selecting a campsite for the night over the course of our trip became an art. I read as much as I could prior to our excursion about others who had cycled long distances. The preference was to stay at a campground. When campgrounds were not available, church grounds and schoolyards seemed to be popular overnight camping locations. In our adventure across southern Colorado and Kansas, town parks were the location of choice. It appeared every town in Kansas had a well-maintained park, complete with shade trees, restrooms, a water source, and one other thing that was extremely important to us—a playground.

We left Carrollton after a camp-stove–cooked breakfast of apple-cinnamon oatmeal, and we felt sufficiently nourished as we began our day of cycling. My rear wheel kept weighing on my mind, though. I broke another spoke a few miles from the fairgrounds and had to do another emergency road repair. I knew I had to find a bicycle shop soon with the capability to rebuild my rear wheel. Youngstown was up ahead, and I thought a city of approximately 50,000 people should have a bicycle shop that could provide that service. We kept cycling, and I kept praying my rear wheel would hold up.

My stress level increased as we cycled along Route 9 toward Youngstown, Ohio. The road was congested, and I knew we would hit heavier traffic as we made our way closer to Youngstown. The rural roads of Kentucky and western Ohio had spoiled us. It had been nice to cycle without holding a taut line along the edge of the highway with cars moving past us, only inches away. There were certain points along the way that we simply had to accept the hand we were dealt with and grind it out. I guess that is the essence of resiliency, not giving up—no matter the challenge.

Just past Salem, Ohio, as we were chugging along, I noticed that an old, beat-up, sun-bleached pickup truck had been following us for about a quarter of a mile. Suddenly the truck swerved around us, drove up on the shoulder of the road blocking our path, and slammed on the brakes. The driver jumped out and began waving his arms in the air like a wild man, shouting, "Stop! Stop!" All I could think was, *My God, we've been cycling for over 3,000 miles, and finally, we meet one of the nuts my friends warned me about.* But this guy was not a nut at all. He was one of the nicest men I have ever met. As he was driving along, he had noticed Stephen riding in his trailer. Seeing Stephen looking out from the trailer with a smile on his face prompted this man to stop. As he walked up to me, I still did not know what to expect. He reached out and pressed a 10-dollar bill into my hand. I couldn't believe it. He said he knew disposable diapers could be expensive, and he wanted to assist. I am not sure, but I think he had read Marty Minor's newspaper article in the *Herald* from Circleville and saw my comment about the greatest expense of the trip being clean diapers.

This is how Charles Petrarca entered our lives. He was 70 years old, retired, and couldn't part with the pickup truck he had been driving for 27 years. He said it was the first new vehicle he had ever owned, and he wasn't going to part with it any time soon. He pulled away with a wave out of his driver-side window. We were surprised to see him another two miles down the road. He stopped us again and asked if there was anything he could do for us. I told him, as a matter of fact, there was. I did not expect him to have an answer, but I asked in desperation if he knew of a good bicycle shop in the area. Charlie had the answer. He directed us to Boardman, Ohio, a suburb of Youngstown.

The Cycle Sales Company bike shop was a fixture in Boardman. The shop had been around since 1919. Anthony and JoAnn Acierno were the proprietors. We noticed many people going in and out of the shop, purchasing bicycles and gear, and they seemed more like old friends of Anthony and JoAnn rather than customers. As I walked around the bicycle shop, I was hopeful. Ohio had a rich bicycle tradition. Orville and Wilbur Wright were the most famous bicycle mechanics in the world, and they were from right down the road in Dayton.

I asked the bicycle mechanic if he could assist a cross-country cyclist by rebuilding my rear wheel while I waited. I was not disappointed. Within an hour, I had 36 new spokes laced into my rear wheel, and the wheel was running as true as Honest Abe. For good measure, I also ordered two tires for the rear wheels of both my and Berti's bicycles. Because of the drivetrain, rear tires wear out much more quickly than front tires. My newfound friend, Charlie Petrarca, stayed at the bicycle shop throughout the whole process. The bill for rebuilding the wheel and for two bicycle tires came to $40. Charlie paid for all of it. The bicycle shop staff were as surprised as I was. Charlie then walked us across the street to McDonald's and bought lunch for Berti, Stephen, and me.

Call it good fortune, divine intervention, or dumb luck. All I know is that there were critical points throughout the trip when whether we knew it or not, we needed someone to reach out and give us a helping hand. Somehow a guardian angel would always appear. If you cannot place a stitch in time, a guardian angel is the next best thing. As we cycled away from Boardman, we knew we had met another one of those angels, and his name was Charlie.

Chapter Nineteen

KEYSTONE

PENNSYLVANIA'S NICKNAME IS THE KEYSTONE STATE.
Historians will tell you that is because Pennsylvania was the center
of the 13 original colonies. Politicians will tell you Pennsylvania
has taken on the name of the Keystone State because it has been
the center of political and economic developments throughout
the history of America. An argument could be made for that. The
Declaration of Independence was signed in Philadelphia. Our
Constitution was ratified there. Philadelphia was also the nation's
capital for a time. Lincoln delivered his most memorable speech
in the small farm town turned battlefield known as Gettysburg. In
presidential elections, Pennsylvania is an important swing state. It
is difficult to win the presidency without gaining Pennsylvania in
the win column. From an economic perspective, Pennsylvania was
the heart of the steel industry in the 19th and into the 20th century in places like Scranton, Pittsburgh, and Bethlehem, primarily
because of rich iron ore and coal deposits.

Route 304 led us from Youngstown to the village of Hubbard, Ohio,
where Route 304 became Route 318. That is where we crossed the
Pennsylvania state line on August 16th. For Berti, Stephen, and
me, Pennsylvania was not as much a keystone as it was a capstone.
Pennsylvania was our final state. I was several hundred miles from

my hometown, and Berti and Stephen were the same distance from their new home in Moosic.

We cycled into West Middlesex, Pennsylvania, after logging in 35 miles. It was a short day, but we had made good progress over the past two and a half months. In a way, we did not want our whimsical tour to end. I think we may have become "institutionalized." We wanted to attain our goal, but we were apprehensive about ending our adventure where every day was magical. We were uncertain about living a "normal" life again.

We came upon a Catholic church in West Middlesex. We waited well into the evening before pitching our tent, hoping we could find the parish priest so we could ask permission. I made a command decision and pitched our tent as darkening skies were fast upon us. When we awoke behind the Good Shepherd Catholic Church in the morning, we finally found the priest, or more accurately, he found us. He was less than friendly. It occurred to Berti and me that the Protestant ministers we had met along the way were friendlier and more hospitable than the Catholic priests we met. Berti and I were both Catholic, and that assessment disappointed both of us.

Berti and I both had character-developing experiences with the Catholic Church growing up. I was sent to Catholic school in second grade in order to complete First Communion, an important milestone in the Catholic faith. Eucharist, receiving Christ's body and blood in the form of bread and wine, is one of the seven sacraments of the Catholic Church. Second grade at Saint Mary's Catholic School was my first and only year outside of the public-school system. None of my friends attended Saint Mary's School. I was an outsider for the entire year as far as my Catholic schoolmates were concerned. The nuns did not make my life any easier. They were strict disciplinarians. I was more afraid of the nuns than I have been of any other group of people in my entire life. Even the Ranger instructors during my time at U.S. Army Ranger School did not put the fear of God in me as those nuns had done.

Berti had her own struggles in Austria. She started training to become a registered nurse at a Catholic nursing school in Braunau, Austria. Berti remained under the strict tutelage of the nuns until she was 20 years old. Berti and her fellow nursing students had to walk through the Austrian town two by two and holding hands. That was not an easy way to meet friends. For certain infractions, breakfast was withheld. On a regular basis, the nuns would visit the student dormitory rooms, and it was all about; *inspect, detect,* and *reject.* Berti never served in the U.S. military, but she certainly had many of the same basic training experiences.

In all seriousness, Berti and I were loyal Christians. We knew clergy, regardless of their denomination, meant well. Our faith was an important part of our lives, and we knew we had a great deal to be thankful for.

Every region of our country had its own physical challenges and we were learning that western Pennsylvania had hills that rivaled the Ozarks. The western region of Pennsylvania is chock-full of rivers, streams, high ridgelines, and deep valleys. After leaving West Middlesex, we traveled about 25 miles before calling it a day at a KOA near Grove City. We wanted to do some laundry and rest a bit. Our spider-sense worked for us again. It began to rain very hard just after we pitched our tent at our campsite, so we were glad to be off the road. I began to feel under the weather again. This was the third time over the course of our three-month journey that my health began to go south on me. I was beginning to get comfortable with being uncomfortable. That is an important trait to have when you are living out of small packs and sleeping on the ground most nights.

I slithered out of our tent at the Grove City KOA, and I was not feeling any better than I had the night before. However, I had to go on with the show, and I did not want to slow down Berti and Stephen. Before leaving the KOA, I found a payphone and dialed the toll-free phone number for WNEP TV in northeastern Pennsylvania and spoke to a popular reporter from that station,

Mike Stevens. Mike produced a weekly news episode known as *On the Road with Mike Stevens*. He would travel the backroads of northeastern and central Pennsylvania, including the Pocono Mountain region, reporting on unusual people and interesting places. I guess Berti and I qualified as unusual people. Mike said he tentatively would link up with us somewhere along Route 208 and shoot some film for a story he wanted to run about our trip. I thought to myself, *I am sure he will show, especially if it is a slow news day.*

We followed Route 208 much of the day. We hit hair-raising speeds as we negotiated a steep black diamond slope plummeting into the town of Emlenton. After months on the road, we easily mastered the descent. As we cycled through Emlenton, we stopped to take in the magnificent sight of the Emlenton truss bridge spanning the Allegheny River on Interstate 80. When it was constructed in 1968, the bridge gained notoriety as the highest bridge within the interstate highway system.

We had to work hard to reach the town of Clarion. We took a wrong turn before entering Clarion and went about six miles out of our way. This was not the first time this had happened. We were pretty good at reading maps, but in 1983, we did not have GPS as a backup. Not only did we log extra mileage, but as a bonus, we got caught in the rain. When we reached the outskirts of Clarion, we were treated to a long climb before we entered the college town. Clarion was a picturesque town, and its centerpiece was a 19th-century courthouse. From a distance, it looked more like a church with a red brick steeple extending high in the air. A prison was built at the rear of the courthouse, making it a full-service facility.

Venturing a few blocks from the courthouse, we came to the campus of Clarion University. The college, like the town, also dated to the 19th century. The town of Clarion had about 2,000 residents. The university had over double that number of students attending undergraduate and graduate classes. We decided to spend the night at the university. We found the Theta Chi fraternity house, and the students there welcomed us to stay with them for the evening.

Leadership development, personal development, and service are the cornerstones of the chapter. The fraternity members were easy-going. They were very interested in our trip and what we had seen, where we had stayed, and whom we had met. They were amazed by Stephen, and they loved his orange covered trailer. I think we ignited the lust for adventure in many of them. Besides having a cheerful group of young people to talk to, we also had a hot shower and a thickly carpeted floor to sleep on. I would choose a dry, soft floor over soggy, lumpy ground every time.

We awoke at the frat house at Clarion University and treated our-selves to breakfast at the McDonald's down the street. Before leaving Clarion, I called WARM radio and spoke to Jerry Heller, providing another progress report. Apparently, people back in northeastern Pennsylvania were getting more excited by the day as our trip was nearing its completion. I still felt sick, but I did not let on during the radio interview.

We followed Route 322 east all day until we came to the Bobette Motel, just east of Reynoldsville. We needed to be good to our-selves, or at least I needed to be good to myself, and Berti and Stephen were okay with that. We found ourselves a comfortable little room complete with a shower, bed, and television. It was about the simple things in life. The hotel manager dug up a tricycle, and Stephen raced around the parking lot, completing around 20 laps. It was nice to see his little legs spinning in circles for a change. Berti and I had logged 35 miles for the day, and Stephen probably biked two miles on his tricycle. It was a big parking lot.

The next morning, we cycled away from the Bobette Motel in Reynoldsville and continued east on Route 322. The terrain was not difficult, but the traffic was heavy. As we cycled along, I heard a familiar snap and felt a tug at my rear-brake caliper. I coasted to the side of the road, and upon inspection, I saw that I had broken another spoke on my rear wheel, opposite the freewheel side. I was getting pretty good at these emergency road repairs. I replaced the spoke, trued the wheel, and we were on our way again.

109

We cycled into the Morrisdale-Philipsburg region and met Jack Killian and his wife, Elva Mae. Jack was a salesman at a Dodge dealership in Clearfield. As Jack was driving from his job in Clearfield to his home in Morrisdale, he saw us cycling along Route 322. Jack arrived at his home and discussed his strange sighting with Elva Mae. They then drove out to meet us along the road, probably to see just how strange we really were, as they contemplated inviting us to spend the night with them. We must have done well enough during our roadside interview and gained an invitation for a night's stay at Casa Killian. We gladly accepted their kind offer to camp in their backyard, take a shower, and share a meal.

Jack was a gregarious man, and he and his wife were excited to hear our stories of how we had made our way across the country. Like most people, they took a liking to Stephen and were amazed at how healthy and happy he was after spending months on the road. Jack contacted Dolly Killion, a reporter from the *Clearfield Progress* newspaper, to interview Berti and me. Dolly came by to conduct the interview and snapped pictures of Stephen and his trailer. She wrote a comprehensive article about our trip that appeared in the newspaper the following day.

Our ride through the Keystone State was turning out well. Berti and I realized that our cycling adventure was rapidly coming to its successful conclusion. We estimated we had about another week on the road. We began to reflect on our ride of a lifetime. We had not known what to expect when we began our unusual trip from Tacoma, Washington, months ago. The best memories we had were from the people we had met. We were kindred spirits with the other cross-country travelers we met along the way. Everyone had their own reasons for taking on the challenge of cycling across the United States. Most made the trek with a sense of adventure in their hearts. Many relished the physical challenge. Both reasons probably applied to us. To be honest, I cannot really say what drew me to wanting to make the trip with my family. I think it was the romanticism of crossing our nation under our power—no man-made engine or gasoline, but rather legs, lungs, and heart, fueled by the calories we consumed and our goal of reaching Moosic.

Embarking on an adventure like ours takes faith. We had faith in one another as members of a family unit. We had faith in a power greater than ourselves to reach down and provide protection and assistance when we did not have the means to protect or assist ourselves. The Higher Power we had faith in never let us down.

Chapter Twenty

FAMILY REUNION

FAMILIES ARE SPECIAL. MY FAMILY WAS THE PRIMARY reason Berti and I made the decision to leave the Pacific Northwest and move across the country to northeastern Pennsylvania. My dad was getting older and I wanted to spend time with him. I was the youngest of seven children, with two sisters and four brothers. All of them lived in the same neighborhood where we grew up and worked in the business my father founded after he returned home from World War II. Berti and I were not traveling to Moosic, Pennsylvania as much as we were traveling back to my roots.

Jack Killian shared route recommendations as we packed our kit and prepared to move closer to my hometown of Moosic. He suggested we cycle along Routes 53, 144, 220, and then 150. We concurred. Jack and Elva Mae gave Stephen one last hug before we buckled him into his orange coach. It was a warm Sunday morning, August 21st as Berti, Stephen, and I traveled along the north rim of the Black Moshannon Forest. It seemed like the tall pine trees waved at us as the wind blew through their boughs. The Black Moshannon State Forest is one of the prettiest places on earth. It sits in the center of Pennsylvania. The Seneca tribe used the area as fishing and hunting grounds centuries ago. On maps, you can still see the outline of a Native American trail. The forest appears today much as it might have looked when Native Americans ruled the land. The Black Moshannon State Park is the centerpiece of the forest, with a large bog surrounded by tall pine trees and rugged ridgelines. The riding was very hilly and demanding, but the scenery sustained us.

We planned to stay at Bald Eagle State Park, near the town of Howard. However, our plans were dashed, but for good reason. We were in a general store in Howard when we noticed a car towing a pop-up camper coming to a halt in the parking lot. Out stepped the Mozeleski family; my sister Ruthie, her husband, Rich, and their sons, Bryan and David. They had been driving along the road hoping to spot us. As they drove past the general store, our bicycles caught their eye. Not too many other cyclists had a large orange trailer attached to a bicycle. Our bicycles were a dead giveaway. After hugs and kisses, they suggested we spend the night camping together. It was a grand idea. Because they had a camper, we could not stay at Bald Eagle State Park where tent camping was the only kind of camping allowed. The Liberty Sportsman Campground was the next best choice.

Berti and I cycled past Bald Eagle State Park, a few miles farther east on Route 150, to link up with my sister and her family at the Liberty Sportsman Campground. We logged in 55 miles on a very scenic day of cycling, but the best thing I saw all day was Ruthie and her family. Berti, Stephen, and I spent the evening and the next day with my sister's family swapping stories, swimming, and "pigging out" together on campfire fare, with the mountains of central Pennsylvania as a backdrop.

Ruthie, Rich, and the kids said farewell around 7 p.m. that second evening. It was not a sad farewell. Berti and I knew that we would be home in a few days. They were very proud of what we had accomplished, but like most other members of my family, they could not really understand why we had engaged in such an undertaking.

Later that evening, Vi and Harv, the campground owners, came by to visit. Harv gave Stephen a long tractor ride through the camp.

Harv had as big a grin on his face as Stephen had as they traversed the campground on the green tractor, the motor sputtering as they rode. Harv was happy we shared Stephen with him for the evening, and I could tell that Vi and Harv loved the campground life. Before we said goodnight, Vi and Harv invited us to their house at the campground. Over evening coffee, Berti and I shared stories of the trail once traveled, along with the trail we hoped to travel once we settled in northeastern Pennsylvania. The next morning, we left Vi and Harv's sportsman's camp and continued east on Route 150.

We reached Lock Haven around noon on August 23rd on what turned out to be a busy day. Jeff Fleishman, a reporter from the Lock Haven newspaper, snagged us when we entered the town. Jeff found Stephen sleeping soundly in what he christened a "covered wagon." After the interview and pictures, Jeff wrote an article that appeared in the *Lock Haven Express* newspaper. Over 20 articles about our trip appeared in the newspapers of small towns and cities over the course of our three months on the road. I hoped that our story would inspire others, as others had inspired us throughout our journey.

After the interview with Jeff, two strangers stopped us. These ladies were all smiles as they spotted Stephen. They were in their mid-60's and had that grandmotherly look about them. Mrs. Malcolm Packer, from Park Street in Lock Haven, and her friend Esther Galbraith, visiting from Seneca, New York, insisted on buying us lunch. Our hungry stomachs would not allow us to turn them down. Now that we were in my home state, it seemed as though people were expecting us, and they took a great deal of pleasure in buying us lunch or inviting us into their homes. I think the publicity we were getting from WARM radio piqued public interest. WARM was known as the "Mighty 590" because of its significant reach, and it claimed channel 590 on the AM dial. WARM was one of the most powerful stations in northeastern Pennsylvania, its frequency reaching the center of the state from the Scranton/Wilkes-Barre area in northeast Pennsylvania.

Before leaving Lock Haven, a news crew from WBRE TV caught up with us. WBRE is a local station I grew up watching as a kid. The television crew wanted to take shots of my legs straining to pull Stephen and his trailer up a long hill, and I must have lugged Stephen up that hill at least five times until the camera angle was just right. The news crew also made comments about how our colorful array of gear was perfect for television. It was not lost on Berti and me that we had the appearance of a circus coming into town. I guess bright-yellow packs strapped to bicycles with a large orange trailer tagging along will have that effect.

By day's end, we cycled into Hughesville after a 60-mile day on the hilly and rural roads of central Pennsylvania. Berti and I had a good first impression of Hughesville, the type of town that seemed like a perfect place to raise a family. It was a place where people drove Chevrolets, ate apple pie, and had an American flag flying from their front porches. Hughesville was also home to the Lycoming County Fair, which had been celebrated for over 100 years. We cycled to the Hughesville Methodist Church. I found the pastor and asked him if we could camp alongside the church. The pastor told me he did not mind but recommended a town park where he thought we would be more comfortable. In the meantime, a local resident, Jim Andrews, came by with a loaf of zucchini bread for us. When he heard how the conversation was going, he promptly and emphatically said, "I have a big house. You can stay there with us tonight." Jim's invitation was welcomed, and his house sounded much better than the town park.

That is how Jim and Judy Andrews came to be our hosts in Hughesville. Jim was not kidding about having a large house. Berti and I could feel a warmth throughout the spacious home due to the décor and the big hearts of the owners. Jim owned a micro-engraving business. He could micro-engrave anything of value–hunting rifles, bicycles, antiques. The engraving could not be seen with the naked eye, appearing as a scratch, but a magnifying glass would allow one to read the engraving. Jim could engrave a name onto an item, that if stolen, would allow the rightful owner to identify the item if it was recovered. Jim was very proud of his business and pointed out that it took special equipment and skill to etch this unique kind of engraving. We spent a comfortable evening together, enjoying dinner and watching the television story about our bicycle adventure on WBRE. Jim and Judy enjoyed the news segment as much as we did, feeling they had bona fide celebrities as their guests. The delicious dinner Judy prepared, followed by an equally appealing breakfast the next morning, was exactly what we needed to continue the trip. Judy even provided calories to go, giving us two more loaves of fresh, homemade zucchini bread for the road.

That morning we chugged along Route 118 with no choice but to plug away through the steep hills that come with the stunning scenery of Pennsylvania. Near the town of Red Rock and Ricketts Glen State Park, the ridgelines become frequent and tough to climb. Rickets Glen is one of Pennsylvania's most scenic areas. Every season produces its own magic at the park. The park's trail is surrounded by waterfalls that glisten in the sun during summer and are shrouded in ice during winter.

WNEP TV reporter Mike Stevens and his camera crew met us near Red Rock. We were happy to be the subject of another local news story. As far as we were concerned, ours was an inspirational story. Unlike many of the stories seen on the news, which focus on crime and misfortune, we felt that our story was uplifting. Ours was a unique tale. This was the first time the reporters who covered our journey had encountered parents venturing across the country with two bikes, a trailer, and their baby.

We ended the day at Good's Campground near Rickets Glen. We logged in 30 miles through pristine woodland on this short day of cycling. The evening was special, as we enjoyed another family reunion with my sister Ann and her family. It was fun to reconnect with Ann and her children, especially over a campfire. We left Good's Campground the next morning and cycled a congested route into the city of Wilkes-Barre along Routes 118, 309, and

11. Berti and I had to negotiate tricky downhill terrain the last few miles into Wilkes-Barre before spending the evening at one of Wilkes-Barre's finest hotels, known as the Station. Just as the name implied, the Station highlighted the rich locomotive legacy of the region.

I enjoyed the best family reunion of the past few days when my dad came to see Berti, Stephen, and me at the Station that evening, accompanied by his longtime friend, Laura Ostrowski. It was a wonderful experience to introduce Stephen to his paternal grandfather for the first time. The family reunion continued later in the evening when my brother Jerry visited along with my sisters, Ruthie and Ann. We were almost home.

The next day, August 26th, we enjoyed a short bicycle ride over terrain I was very familiar with from Wilkes-Barre to West Pittston. We spent the evening in West Pittston at the home of my brother Jerry's in-laws. This would be our last night spent on the road. The next day, we planned to reach our destination, Moosic, Pennsylvania. Some people say you can never go home again. I was going to try.

Chapter Twenty-One

Homecoming

I LEFT MY HOMETOWN OF MOOSIC, PENNSYLVANIA IN
October 1978 to join the Army and I served at Fort Benning,
Georgia, and Fort Lewis, Washington. Life had changed dramatically. I left home single and returned a married man with a young
son. Berti and I had visited Moosic in the summer of 1980 as we
were moving from Georgia to Washington. Now we were on our
way back to Moosic and we planned to stay for a while. What a
homecoming it turned out to be.

We awoke in West Pittston, Pennsylvania, on Saturday, August 27th.
This day would mark the final day of our cross-country adventure.
I wished Berti a happy 28th birthday. We could not have planned
Berti's birthday celebration any better if we had tried. It was spe-
cial in that we would be culminating our great adventure and cel-
ebrating Berti's birthday on the same day.

Ten miles to home. This would be the shortest ride of our last
three months on the road. We cycled through the town of Pittston,
home of the annual Tomato Festival, and then through the towns
of Hughestown and Duryea. Motorists blew their horns and people
waved from front porches all along this last portion of our route.
It was a short ride to reach the borough line of Moosic, where we
were forced to stop. Mayor Frank Assaf was there to greet us. He

shook my hand, hugged Berti, and waved at Stephen, who sat quietly in his trailer.

We continued through Moosic along Route 11, moving toward the Greenwood section of town where my father's business stood. My dad, Paul Xavier Gronski Sr., was raised by his mother, a Polish immigrant. My grandmother never learned to speak English well. She owned a small grocery store, selling primarily candy and cigarettes. My paternal grandfather, also a Polish immigrant, died in an accident in the coal mines near Scranton when my grandmother was five months pregnant with my dad. The son of a single parent, my father was forced to quit school after the seventh grade so he could work and help support the family.

My dad served overseas during World War II in the US Army Air Corps. Dad opened a garage in 1954 doing minor car repairs and selling used tires. Soon he bought cars to fix up and sell, and so began his venture into the used car business. His family and his business were growing. But dad, and my entire family faced a devasting setback in 1956 when my mother passed away when I was very young. Dad became a single parent with seven children to raise and a business to run. It was a severe blow, but dad fought through it. By outward measures, my father was unimpressive. Standing five feet, six inches tall, dad weighed about 135 pounds. But my dad was a grinder and he had the blood of an entrepreneur. Through sheer hard work and desire, he raised his children while building an enterprise that included a garage, used car sales, a towing service, a boat sales and service business, and a bike shop. Known as Paul Gronski Enterprises Inc., dad's business became a landmark in northeastern Pennsylvania. Paul X. Gronski Sr., a man with only a seventh-grade education, became a pillar of the community and a leader in his church.

Our trip would culminate at the family business. About three blocks from our destination our ride came to a dead stop. We were greeted by the Riverside High School marching band. I graduated from Riverside High School in 1974. It was heartwarming to see the band from my alma mater participate in our welcome home parade. Hundreds of people lined the street. Route 11, a major artery through Moosic, was shut down. Cars were detoured around the entire town. Everyone wanted to shake our hands and give us a hug. Of course, everyone wanted to see Stephen. Our son was the center of attention at the start of our adventure, and he was the center of attention during the trip. He remained the center of attention now as our ride across America came to an end. There was a wave of well-wishers swelling around our bicycles. After cycling over 4,000 miles, Berti and I walked our bicycles the last three blocks of the journey.

According to the *Scranton Times* newspaper, Berti, Stephen, and I were greeted by about 1,000 people, a marching band, and a police escort. The Scranton Boys Club was also there to greet us. They joined the parade with three young Boys Club members carrying a banner, followed by the Boys Club executive director riding in a shiny sedan. Our fund-raising effort for the Scranton Boys Club was a success. People far and wide donated money to the Boys Club in response to the sweat we put into our journey. Dick Fleck, a longtime family friend and race car enthusiast, raised money in honor of our trip on behalf of the Boys Club and presented a check to us as we dismounted our bicycles.

It was kind of like a version of the television show *This Is Your Life*. Friends and neighbors I had not seen in years were there to greet us. Tears came to my eyes. The parade, the party, and the home-coming were all overwhelming. I was happy for Berti and especially happy for Stephen, who garnered most of the attention. My father had a 16-inch-wheel bicycle picked out for Stephen. Dad gave Stephen a big hug, sat him atop the new bike, and happily pushed his grandson around the area in front of the business. After traveling for months with only his mom and dad and an occasional cross-country cyclist or two, Stephen was confused by the throngs of people, but he warmed up quickly to everyone.

Stephen was dressed for the occasion. He had traveled across the United States with two pairs of shorts and one pair of sweatpants. The necessity of traveling light meant we could not have extravagant wardrobes. The night before our homecoming, Stephen received a new outfit, appropriate for a parade grand marshal. He wore a white shirt with sporty blue shorts and white knee socks.

It was a proud day for my dad, a man of the World War II era, and a member of the "greatest generation." Dad was used to staying in his lane and working hard. Cycling across the United States was a foreign concept for him. Still, he knew we had accomplished something difficult and unusual. Dad knew this was something big. Being a World War II veteran, he had always wanted me to serve in the military, and he was proud that I served in the Army and achieved the rank of captain. My dad was a businessman and a marketer. He not only wanted to communicate to everyone that I had served in the military, but he also wanted to put in a plug for Ross Bicycles. He had a banner made and strung across the busy highway in front of his business. It read "Welcome Home CAPT. John L. Gronski, Berti, & Stephen, Crossing the USA On A Ross Bike."

Several newspapers, radio stations, and television stations were there as our trip came to a happy conclusion. We gained international attention when a newspaper in Austria picked up the story. I was quoted in one newspaper as saying, "I don't think there's one thing that really stands out. It's just how nice the people were all along the way." That really is what life is all about. It is about people, family, friends.

Not many families can experience a celebration like we did that Saturday morning on August 27, 1983. Berti, Stephen, and I celebrated with my dad and all my brothers and sisters; Paul Jr., Ruthie, Ann, Jerry, Robert, and Jimmy. Their families were there too. Stephen was greeted by approximately 20 cousins he had never met before. It was indeed a homecoming.

Chapter Twenty-Two

TRANSFORMATION

BY ANY STANDARD, OUR CROSS-COUNTRY BICYCLE adventure was transformational for Berti and me. The experience took us out of our comfort zone. We entered the adventure with our entire minds, bodies, and souls. We faced uncertainty and accepted risk. We had to think clearly and make multiple decisions daily that affected our well-being and Stephen's safety. We maintained positive attitudes, even in the face of adversity. Berti and I pushed through physical pain and illness throughout our time on the road. The weather and topography added to the physical strain. Our experiences, throughout the course of our trip, affected us deeply on an emotional level. We had to face feelings about ourselves and about each other, and there was no place to run. The people we encountered and the scenery we saw added to our emotional experience. We placed our faith in a power greater than ourselves and that higher power never let us down. The physical, emotional, and spiritual experiences were powerful. Our journey created memories that have lasted us a lifetime and we were blessed in that our son Stephen accounted for many of those memories. We learned lessons and gained confidence. The adventure took place while we were in our formative years as a family and we grew stronger. Yes, this cross-country bicycle adventure was a transformational experience.

Why?

People ask, "Why this adventure? Why take on such an audacious challenge with a wife and baby?" I still search for answers. There was something about making the trip across the United States by bicycle, using only human power, that excited me. The physical challenge, the scenery, the camping, and conducting the trip self-supported were compelling. I was also looking forward to meeting average Americans as we made the journey, and we were heartened by the people we encountered. It is easy to meet people when you are on a bicycle. On a bicycle you are exposed, unlike people encapsulated in a car, and strangers seem to be less intimidated to approach a cyclist than they are someone perched atop a 1250cc Harley. You are vulnerable on a bicycle, and that vulnerability draws people in. Conducting our cross-country bike trip as a family made the experience even more special. Berti agreed to take the adventure with me, and we simply never saw Stephen as an obstacle. He was part of the team.

What?

People ask, "What did you learn?" We learned a great deal about life, leadership, and love.

Life

Follow your dreams. When it comes to following your dreams, find ways to say yes, but acknowledge the nos. There are not many dreams worth pursuing that do not have obstacles standing in the way. People will tell you why you cannot achieve your goal. Some of these warnings are warranted, but that should not stop you. Recognize the obstacles that stand in the way of your dream, and then work hard to reduce those impediments. Harness the positive energy required to start your journey, and fight through the challenges in order to reach the finish line. Every journey begins with a single step. Do not take counsel of your fears. Take that first step. Just make sure you have prepared the ground.

Start slow and learn as you go. U.S. Army Rangers are taught something known as SLLS (pronounced "sills"). SLLS stands for Stop, Look, Listen, Smell. About 10 minutes into a patrol, Rangers learn to stop and observe their environment. They take in the sounds and smells around them in order to become aware of their surroundings. They look for anything unusual. They also adjust equipment before continuing. Berti and I did the same thing after the first day of our long trip across the country. We kept our first leg to only 30 miles and then took the time to adjust our equipment and reorient ourselves. In the U.S. Army we also learn that when we take on a new leadership position, we should observe and ask questions before making drastic changes. Start slow and learn, rather than starting fast and rushing to failure.

A team tackling a challenge together becomes stronger. Working to overcome adversity builds resilience and promotes growth. A team, whether it be a husband and wife, a football team, or an army infantry squad, strengthen their bond after going through a crucible event together. Confidence develops and trust grows. We found that the challenges of the steep hills, snow-covered mountains, cold rain, hot sun, strong winds, insects, and beasts tested us, and we became stronger. We became stronger as individuals and stronger as a team. Our marriage became stronger as a result of the challenges we faced together. If you want to go fast, go alone. If you want to go far, go together.

There is no reward without risk. Seldom is anything good attained without struggle and without assuming prudent risk. The key is to take steps to mitigate the risk. Thorough preparation is one way to mitigate risk.

Nature nurtures the soul. For the three months we cycled across the country, we were amid nature and gorgeous scenery. Through the Cascades, the red canyons of eastern Oregon, the Snake River, the Great Salt Lake region, the Rockies, the amber waves of grain, the Ozarks, woodland forests, lakes, and streams, we saw God's most beautiful creations. The scenery had a calming effect and caused our spirits to soar. Even while struggling to negotiate terrain associated with this beauty, we were at peace. Being one with nature is rejuvenating and is a form of meditation.

It is all about the journey, and the journey never ends. Our trip was not necessarily about our destination, but rather, it was about what we experienced—the people we met, the beauty we saw, and what we learned. It also comes down to how you negotiate the trail. You cannot check your values and principles at the door. You must adhere to your values, especially when the going gets tough. Once you achieve your goal, it is then about figuring out what is next. If you are not moving forward, time passes you by and you move backward. Once you scale one summit, you must find another to climb.

Leadership

Character, competence, and resilience are essential for effective leadership. Leaders must be true to their values even when their backs are against the wall. Leaders must cultivate trust by trusting others first, sharing the load, and following through on promises. Leaders must care more about those they lead than they care about themselves. Leaders must clearly communicate a vision or action plan that is realistic and believable, be problem solvers, and have the courage to make decisions. Leaders must help others develop and become stronger, and leaders must be fit in many ways, including physical, spiritual, mental, and emotional fitness. Leaders must have the resilience to overcome adversity. Resiliency is not only about toughness, but is also about exuding positive energy that inspires others. Having a positive attitude is essential. We choose how we feel. We can choose to be happy or sad, angry or calm, upbeat or down. Organizations and teams take on the attitude and personality of their leaders. The attitudes of those on a team reflect the leader's attitude. If your team has a bad attitude, look in the mirror.

Purpose is powerful. A leader must clearly communicate purpose. "Why" trumps "what" every time. A sense of purpose inspires a team to fight through challenges that stop others who are not working toward a meaningful goal.

Rehearsals are crucial to successful execution. We conducted several trial runs with Stephen and his trailer before we launched our trip. Every trial run taught us lessons about how to improve the trailer to enhance Stephen's safety. After starting out slowly the first day of our trip, we learned to distribute weight to improve the performance of the ride. Look before you leap.

Good followership is as important as good leadership in order to have a team function smoothly. Followers have the responsibility *to do their job*. Everyone on a team has a role to play. It is incredible how well a team functions when everyone focuses on the job they must do. A well-known quote reads, "It is amazing how much could be accomplished when no one cares who gets the credit." Good followers support the leader as well as their teammates. A follower should speak up and offer their opinion, but once a leader decides, it is up to a follower to either follow the plan wholeheartedly or leave the team. Good followers never openly criticize their leaders, but rather speak privately to their leaders if they have a concern. Good followers do not openly criticize teammates but will take a teammate off to the side and discuss issues privately.

A leader must be humble. No leader has all the answers. A leader must have an open mind and be willing to learn from others on the team, even a team member who appears to be less experienced. Everyone on the team has something to offer, and a leader must guide the team with an open mind and eyes wide open. When time permits, a leader should solicit feedback from the team before making important decisions. Leaders who think they have nothing more to learn, learn nothing more. Humility is an important quality in a leader. A leader should never think they are more important than any other team member.

We had to be willing to learn from our mistakes throughout the course of our trip. We had to evaluate how we were responding to situations and adjust accordingly. We all must take time to reflect. Successful coaches understand how to adjust at halftime. The United States Army has perfected the after-action review in order to identify what works well, what must be improved, and what lessons were learned. Learning lessons are not enough. We must apply the lessons we learn.

Love

The innocence of babies and small children opens hearts and doors. Isaiah 11:16 reads, "The wolf also shall dwell with the lamb, the leopard shall lie down with the young goat, the calf and the young lion and the fatling together; and a little child shall lead them." During our adventure, Stephen softened the hearts of many people we met, who then aided us in our journey. We were led as much by the aura that surrounded Stephen as he was led by us.

We learned not to judge others by their position or their appearance. Just because a person holds a lofty position does not mean they are virtuous, and just because a person has a scraggly beard and long hair does not mean they are worthless. Be careful to judge people by what they have in their hearts, souls, and minds before you judge them based on their looks or their station in life.

When you are nice to people, people are nice to you. We learned the power of karma. Intent and actions influence the future. There are no good results without good effort. My father used to say, "The world doesn't owe you a living." What you sow is what you reap. People who help others are usually happy and successful. Peter Drucker, an Austrian born American management consultant said, "Do not focus on being successful; focus on being useful." You will succeed if you focus on helping others succeed.

Take time to give thanks, and do not be afraid to show love. Two of the most important words in the English language are *thank you*. Show gratitude for what people provide and for what our Creator has blessed us with. Use words of love. When you are proud of someone, let them know that. Let the ones you love know that you love them. Telling those you love that you love them and that you are proud of them is very powerful. Along with loving words, ensure you demonstrate loving deeds. Do nice things for people even when they do not ask you to.

The best pleasures in life are simple pleasures. We can take enjoyment from simple things. A hot cup of coffee on a cold morning, a sun setting over the mountains, a cool stream flowing down a hillside, a raptor soaring overhead, a conversation with a newfound acquaintance or an old friend, the hug of a child or a loved one—these are the things that enrich life.

Transformation

During the ride of our lives, we learned lessons about life, leadership, and love, and those lessons have lasted us a lifetime. We were out on the open road for three months, exposed to challenges such as uncertainty, strangers, mechanical breakdowns, health issues, cold, heat, snow, rain, sun, hills, and wind. Our bicycle trip was a transformational experience. Through this transformational process, we became stronger as individuals and stronger as a family.

The transformation we experienced during our bicycle trip was a microcosm of the evolution we would experience over our lifetime. Through our fantastic journey, we gained self-confidence, and our trust in one another was strengthened. Our journey helped us to grow, and we secured tools to successfully overcome future life challenges. We cemented a strong bond and developed a culture of leaving no family member behind. We would inherently circle the wagons as a family when a family member was faced with adversity.

Transformational leaders are leaders who can effectively communicate a vision, build teams, develop others, and care more about those they lead than they care about themselves. Because of these traits, transformational leaders can transform an organization from what it is into something better. But there is another element to transformational leadership. Transformational leaders are self-aware. They are never satisfied with their current maturity level as a leader, but always seek ways to grow and develop to become an even stronger leader.

Our bicycle journey was a key transformational event. The experience and growth we realized during our cross-country adventure established a rock-solid foundation as we continued our journey through life. We have continued to grow and transform. Here is to growth! Here is to transformation!

About the Author

John L. Gronski retired from the United States Army as a major general after more than 40 years of service on active duty and in the Pennsylvania National Guard. John is a combat veteran of the Iraq War, having commanded a brigade in Ramadi, Iraq, from 2005 to 2006. Other significant assignments included Deputy Commanding General, National Guard, US Army Europe and Commanding General of the 28th Infantry Division. John's military training includes the U.S. Army War College, the Infantry Officer Advanced Course, Ranger School, and Airborne School. He has numerous military awards, including the Distinguished Service Medal with oak leaf cluster, the Legion of Merit with oak leaf cluster, the Bronze Star, and the Combat Infantry Badge. He has also received awards from the countries of Poland and Lithuania.

John is the founder and CEO of Leader Grove Consulting, LLC, a leadership and management consulting firm; a senior mentor for the U.S. Army Mission Command Training Program; and an adjunct Fellow with the Center for European Policy Analysis. John earned an MBA from Penn State University and a master's in strategic studies from the U.S. Army War College. John attended Alvernia University as a doctoral student in the corporate leadership program. He has been certified as a project management professional, and he holds a master certificate as a Lean Six Sigma Black Belt from Villanova University.

John is a transformational leader. He is an adherent of character-based servant leadership. John has strategic and operational experience at senior levels in both the military and civilian sectors and has led small teams and large complex organizations. John's personal leadership philosophy is built upon character, competence, and resilience. He believes that everyone can develop as a stronger leader. John is a much sought-after speaker and leadership consultant. His presentations feature inspirational stories and wisdom gained from his own leadership experience and the experience of others. John's life purpose is to positively influence others to become virtuous people and leaders through his mentoring and through his example.

John and his wife Berti were married in 1980 and are the proud parents of Stephen and Timothy. John and Berti continue to enjoy outdoor activities and enjoy spending time with family and friends.

Contact John at:

Email: GronskiJ15@gmail.com or JohnGronski@LeaderGrove.com
Twitter: @JLGronski
Website: www.LeaderGrove.com
LinkedIn: https://www.linkedin.com/in/john-gronski

CPSIA information can be obtained
at www.ICGtesting.com
Printed in the USA
LVHW020723301220
675397LV00005B/267